PENGUIN BOOKS

MICROWAVE COOKING FOR BABIES AND TODDLERS

VIRGINIA HILL became a microwave demonstrator with the Sharp Corporation in 1977. She soon realised that there was a need for more consumer education on microwave cooking and established her own consultancy, the Microwave Cooking Centre, in 1980.

To reach a larger audience than she could through her classes, in 1982 she produced *The All Australian Microwave Recipe Book* and an accompanying video. She has since had a number of books published. Her *Microwave Tips and Techniques* was published by Penguin Books Australia in 1991 and reprints regularly. In 1992 she published *Virginia Hill's Microwave Companion* (Viking O'Neil), an encyclopaedia of microwave cooking, which met with critical acclaim.

KAREN INGE, who provided the dietary advice and nutritional data, is a registered dietitian and a director of The Institute of Health and Fitness and Olympic Park Sports Medicine Centre. She is the co-author of *Food for Sport* and author of *Food, Fitness and Feeling Good*, and she contributes to various publications as well as appearing regularly on television.

MICROWAVE COOKING FOR BABIES AND TODDLERS

Virginia Hill

PENGUIN BOOKS

Penguin Books Australia Ltd
487 Maroondah Highway, PO Box 257
Ringwood, Victoria 3134, Australia
Penguin Books Ltd
Harmondsworth, Middlesex, England
Viking Penguin, A Division of Penguin Books USA Inc.
375 Hudson Street, New York, New York 10014, USA
Penguin Books Canada Limited
10 Alcorn Avenue, Toronto, Ontario, Canada M4V 3B2
Penguin Books (N.Z.) Ltd
182–190 Wairau Road, Auckland 10, New Zealand

First published by Penguin Books Australia Ltd 1993
This edition published by Penguin Books Australia Ltd 1994

10 9 8 7 6 5 4 3 2 1

Typeset in Berner by Midland Typesetters, Maryborough, Victoria
Design by George Dale
Line drawings by Lorraine Ellis
Food preparation (front cover) by Janene Brooks
Printed in Australia by Australian Print Group, Maryborough, Victoria

National Library of Australia
Cataloguing-in-Publication data:

Hill, Virginia.
Microwave cooking for babies and toddlers.

Includes index.
ISBN 0 14 024090 X.

1. Microwave cookery. 2. Cookery (Baby foods). I. Title.

641.5882

Contents

Acknowledgements
My sincere thanks to Kay Caffarella, for practical and creative recipe development assistance; Jack and Jess Caffarella, for tasting the finished recipes; Sister Bev Helmore, Maternal and Child Health Nurse, for manuscript assistance; and Clare Coney, for shepherding us through the shoals of editing without fuss.

Introduction

Microwave ovens make it easy for modern parents to cook fresh, nutritious food for their children quickly. Microwaving is a fast and inexpensive method of cooking dishes so they do not lose their nutrients or flavour and, as an added benefit, microwaving minimises washing up.

As any parent knows, young children can be very demanding, leaving little time for preparing meals and cleaning up afterwards. However, if you use a microwave oven, little effort and expense are needed to prepare good food for your family.

Microwaving is also safer than conventional cooking, for there is no danger of toddlers' fingers getting burnt on a hot oven door, or a saucepan of boiling liquid being knocked off the stove top. Additionally, you can have peace of mind knowing the oven will switch off automatically, even if you have been distracted by a crying child.

Microwaving is ideal for cooking small portions, as the smaller the amount of food in the oven, the faster it cooks. Vegetables can be ready to purée in two or three minutes. Even for family meals, a microwave cooks on average two-thirds faster than a conventional stove, saving time and electricity, while there is no problem with baked-on residues.

When you are cooking for small children, it isn't worth spending an hour making an elaborate recipe. One day the child may eat enthusiastically, the next refuse even a mouthful. This is natural, but if you are exhausted by broken nights and have cooked a special meal, you will be upset if you have to throw it away untouched. Aim to cook simple dishes, and use the speed of the microwave to prepare meals quickly.

The time you will save by microwaving can be used to present the food more attractively: a reluctant eater can be interested in food if it is arranged as a picture, for instance a face made of fruit or vegetables.

The most important things to remember when introducing your child to solid food are to make mealtimes enjoyable, and instil habits of healthy eating as early as possible. Try to offer a wide choice of tastes, textures and colours. Use fresh, natural ingredients. If you establish good eating patterns at an early age your child will benefit for the rest of his or her life.

Where the title of a recipe is followed by (F), it is suitable for the whole family to eat, although the child's portion may be removed before adult seasoning and garnishing.

MICROWAVE ESSENTIALS

Using a microwave oven

Microwave ovens cook with power, not heat. When the oven is turned on, electricity is converted into microwave energy – short radio waves of high frequency – by a magnetron tube. The microwaves are directed into the oven where a rotating antenna or stirrer fan distributes them.

Microwaves bounce off the metal walls of the oven. They pass through non-metallic containers such as plastic, ovenable glass, pyro-ceramics or paper, which do not reflect or absorb microwaves, and penetrate food to a depth of up to 4 cm. The molecules of moisture in the food are made to vibrate extremely fast by the microwave energy, and this causes friction which, in turn, produces heat within the food and thus cooks it. If the food is more than 4 cm deep the centre of the food cannot be cooked by the microwaves. Instead it cooks by heat travelling through the food – conduction – as in conventional cooking.

Once the oven is turned off, or the door is opened, there is no possibility of microwaves 'leaking'. The microwaves are no longer being generated. There is no residue of microwaves left inside food cooked in a microwave oven, and microwaves do not cause any structural or chemical changes in food molecules. All microwave ovens sold are subject to stringent safety standards and all foods cooked in them will be safe if the recipe instructions are followed carefully.

Fundamentals for successful microwaving

- Check the *wattage* of your oven first. Microwave ovens vary in their power and the higher the wattage the quicker food will cook. The recipes in this book have been developed on 650–750 watt ovens. If you are using a 500-watt oven you will need to add approximately 10 per cent extra to the cooking time of the recipe.

- Because microwaves are unequally distributed in the oven you must follow the instructions in a recipe for positioning, stirring, rotating or turning food to ensure the dish is cooked evenly.

- Recipes usually give 'standing time' after the food has been removed from the oven. This allows the conduction of heat through the food, and is an important part of the cooking process. Do not skip it. Standing time is approximately one-quarter of oven cooking time. Food is usually covered while standing to retain the heat.

- Since cooking time depends on weight, it is important to weigh food carefully before setting the timer. Microwave cooking is fast, so it is easy to overcook. If you are in doubt always undercook as any dish can be put back in the oven for an extra minute or two at the end.

- Use only microwave-safe cookware and equipment.

- Recipes recommend containers of certain sizes and shapes. If you cook in a different shaped container be aware that the timing and finished dish may alter as a result.

- The starting temperature of food will affect the time needed to cook it. Try to let refrigerated food stand at room temperature for at least 15 minutes before microwaving.

- Just as conventional ovens can be set to hot, moderate or cool temperatures, microwave ovens can be set to different power levels. As a rule of thumb recipes that would be cooked slowly conventionally are cooked on LOW (30–40%) power, while for those conventionally cooked fast and hot HIGH (90–100%) power is appropriate. Many microwave ovens have a specific DEFROST power button, but if you have to programme power levels yourself it is equivalent to 30–35% power.

- You can switch between power levels instantaneously – there is no waiting for the oven to heat up or cool down before cooking.

Microwave cooking

Microwave cooking is unlike conventional cooking in that the size and shape of the food is a factor in how it cooks, as is the type of food it is. Foods that are high in fats and sugars cook very fast in the microwave, and one has to be very careful not to overcook them – recipes including cheese, for instance, should always be cooked on LOW (30–40%) power, to prevent chewy results.

Water also attracts microwaves, and foods containing a lot of water will take longer to cook than drier foods. Vegetables high in moisture, such as zucchini, can be cooked without any added water. Very dry foods, such as meringue and pavlova, conversely do not cook well in the microwave.

Microwaves cook food from the surface in. Therefore small pieces cook faster than larger pieces, matchstick slices of carrot cooking more quickly than a whole carrot. Unevenly shaped food cooks unevenly, with the thinner parts cooking faster than the thicker parts. Thus, to ensure that food cooks at the same rate, all the pieces in the microwave should be the same size and shape.

Where food is an uneven shape, for instance a chicken drumstick, the thinner end should be placed towards the centre of the turntable and the thicker end to the outside. More microwaves fall at the outside of the turntable, so this will help equalise the cooking of the drumstick.

When cooking meat, be aware that bones conduct heat well and will cause the meat close to them to cook more rapidly than boneless parts. For even cooking you should select boneless cuts of meat.

The composition of the food also affects the cooking time. Dense, tight-fibred foods take longer to cook than porous ones of the same size – potatoes will take longer to cook than squash, and a roast will take longer than a meat loaf.

Finally, the cooking time is directly related to the amount being cooked. Larger amounts take longer than smaller ones. If one fish finger takes 1 minute, two fish fingers will take 1½ minutes and three fish fingers 2 minutes 25 seconds. An approximate guide to timing increased quantities is to multiply the initial cooking time by the increased amount of food, then subtract a little to prevent overcooking.

Microwave terms and techniques

Aluminium foil See *Foil*.

Arcing If metal is put in the oven small sparks fly between it and the oven walls when the microwave is on. These sparks can cause damage to the oven. Any metal utensil (some mugs contain metal in their handles) will cause arcing, including plates that have gold or silver trims. The only exception is aluminium, which is safe to use in the microwave, provided the foil does not touch the walls of the oven, and not more than one-third of the food is covered by the foil.

Arranging food To maximise the microwave energy it is important to position food correctly. Place small items of food such as potatoes or muffins in a circle on a flat plate, or around the edge of the turntable with a space between each. Thinner parts of food such as lamb chops should be towards the centre of the turntable and the thicker portions to the outside.

Complementary cooking Describes partial cooking of a dish in the microwave and in the conventional oven.

Conduction The flow of heat from one layer to another. The centre of food cooks by conduction in the microwave.

Cookware Utensils suitable for use in the microwave. These are of different materials to conventional cookware. See 'Microwave utensils', pp. 8–10.

Covering Cook food uncovered in the microwave unless recipe states to cover. If told to cover tightly, use a tight-fitting lid or plastic wrap. If told to cover loosely, use a paper towel, or plastic wrap with one corner open or holes pierced in it, to allow steam to escape.

Defrost Microwaves have a special power level, DEFROST (30–35%), that enables frozen foods to be thawed in minutes.

Elevation To allow microwaves to penetrate food from underneath, and thus ensure more even cooking, food can be elevated using special cookware. Food is also sometimes elevated to allow juices to drain freely.

Flavouring In microwave cooking use less herbs, spices and seasonings than you would in conventional cooking, as the shorter microwave cooking time means their flavours are stronger in the finished dish.

Foil Aluminium foil is the only metal that can be used in microwave ovens. You must ensure the food is not completely covered by the foil (the rule of thumb is no more than one-third foil to two-thirds food), that no foil is touching the sides of the oven, that foil containers are not more than 5 cm deep, and foil-lined lids are removed from containers before microwaving. Food covered by foil will be shielded from the microwaves.

Glass Only use microwave-safe ovenable glass. Never use crystal glass, as this contains lead and may crack during heating.

Magnetron The tube that converts electricity in to microwave energy.

Microware Plastic cookware designed especially for use in microwave ovens. Always follow the manufacturer's advice as to safe temperature limits.

Moisture In many microwave recipes the liquid amount is adjusted, as microwaves are attracted to moisture. Cake recipes are wetter than conventional ones, but vegetables are cooked in a minimum amount of water.

Ovenable paperboard Designed especially for use in microwaves, a heat resistant, disposable paperboard covered with a plasticised coating.

Piercing Food covered by any type of 'skin' must be pierced before microwaving to prevent the food bursting due to the build up of steam inside the casing. Potatoes, sausages and egg yolks are all examples of foods that must be pierced.

Plastic cookware Not all plastics are suitable for microwave cooking. Use only recommended plastics.

Plastic wrap In the microwave use only wrap made from polyvinylidene (PVDC) or polyethylene. Check the carton of the wrap before using – is should be marked 'Microwave safe'. If it is not particles may migrate into the food from the wrap.

Power levels Almost all microwave ovens have flexible power settings, so you can control the percentage of microwave energy entering the oven. Each power level or setting is represented by a percentage of full power.

Reheating Reheat on MEDIUM-HIGH (70–80%) or MEDIUM (50–60%) to prevent the food beginning to cook a second time. Always cover food when reheating to retain moisture. Rice, vegetables and casseroles should be stirred from time to time to distribute heat evenly through the dish.

Roasting rack A microwave utensil used to elevate food in the oven and allow juices to drain away during cooking.

Rotating If an oven does not have a turntable, or if food cannot be stirred satisfactorily, it will need to be rotated in order to ensure even cooking. Each rotation should be one-quarter of a complete circle, i.e. 90 degrees.

Salt Do not sprinkle salt directly on the surface of food to be microwaved, as it will result in the food dehydrating and discolouring.

Sensor A feature on some microwave ovens that gauges the steam or humidity present in the oven and automatically calculates the exact cooking time needed.

Sequence cooking A feature on some ovens that allows several steps to be programmed at the beginning of cooking. The oven will then automatically change the power setting during the cooking process.

Shielding Covering sections of food being cooked in the microwave oven with foil. It prevents overcooking by deflecting the microwaves and is used when cooking pieces of food of uneven size, for instance to cover the legs and wings of poultry, or the thin ends of fish fillets, to prevent them overcooking.

Standing time Microwave recipes include standing time after the dish has come out of the oven. This enables the temperature to equalise through the food and completes the cooking. Standing time is generally about a quarter of the total cooking time.

Stirring Liquid foods should be stirred during cooking in the microwave to ensure the heat is distributed equally through the dish. Stir from the edge towards the centre.

Thermometer Conventional thermometers may not be used in microwave ovens. Special microwave thermometers can be bought – they contain reduced amounts of metal.

Venting Piercing holes in plastic wrap, or leaving a space at the lip of a jug, to allow steam to escape during cooking and prevent a liquid boiling over.

Microwave utensils

Plastic, ovenable glass, pyro-ceramics and pottery that is well-glazed with a non-metallic glaze can all be used as containers for microwave cooking, while china plates can be used for reheating so long as they do not have gold or silver trim. However, I recommend investing in a purpose-made set of durable, microwave-safe plastic cookware.

Plastic cookware cooks food faster than glass or ceramic containers. It withstands the heat of cooking well, without breaking or distorting, but it will become hot to touch once the food starts to give off heat. You should therefore choose a set with handles, so the containers are comfortable to pick up, although it is advisable to use oven gloves after long periods of microwave cooking.

The cookware should include containers of different sizes, as the size and shape of the container will affect how the food cooks. The size of the dish should relate to the amount of food being cooked: small amounts of food in a large container will result in overcooking at the edges or an uncooked centre, while too small a dish will result in food spilling out.

Round containers with flat bottoms and straight sides are the best shape, as microwave energy concentrates in the corners of square containers. Shallow dishes are best for reheating food, or cooking food that needs little stirring. Deeper jugs and dishes are used for soups and casseroles that require stirring to equalise the heat distribution.

To check whether a container is suitable for using for microwave cooking, place it clean and dry on the turntable. Next to it put a glass of water. Microwave both on HIGH (90–100%) for 1 minute. If the container is at all warm it has absorbed microwave energy and is unsuitable for use in microwave cooking.

You should avoid using containers made from the following:

- metal (except aluminium foil), as it causes arcing in the oven, and does not allow microwaves to pass through to the food;
- unglazed pottery, as it absorbs microwave energy, becomes very hot and may crack;
- pottery glazed with a metallic glaze, which will again cause damaging arcing;
- china or glass decorated with metallic patterns;
- crystal glass that contains lead;
- materials that have been glued together, as they may come apart in the microwave oven.

Cookware cupboard suggestions

The following containers will enable you to cook a variety of recipes for your baby successfully and speedily.

Bowls (set of two)	0.2 litre (¾ cup), with lid
Small container	0.7 litre (3 cups), with lid
Medium container	1.2 litres (4½ cups), with lid
Large container	2.5 litres (10 cups), with lid
Jug	1 litre (4 cups)
Spoonwhisk (combines tablespoon measure with a whisk)	
Ovenable-glass jug	0.5 litre (2 cups)
Ovenable-glass jug	1 litre (4 cups)

Cake-ring dish 2.45 litres (9 cups)
Roasting rack
Set of scales, blender, sieve and ice-cream scoop

Further accessories

- Plastic wrap – use only microwave-safe wrap.
- Freezer bags – marked microwave-safe, to allow defrosting and reheating of contents.
- Aluminium foil – various containers and wrap.
- White paper towel – not recycled – to use for short-term reheating and as a loose cover.

Warning Recycled paper products contain impurities that can cause arcing or a small fire. Do not use in microwave.

Useful measurements

Microwave Power Settings

Power	Microwave Heat	Conventional Heat
10–20%	Warm	Cool
30–35%	Defrost	Slow
30–40%	Low	Moderately Slow
50–60%	Medium	Moderate
70–80%	Medium High	Moderately Hot
90–100%	High	Hot

Ready Measurements

1 cup	250 ml
1 tablespoon	20 ml
1 teaspoon	5 ml

(All spoon measurements are level.)

Cup Measures (1 cup = 250 ml)

	grams	ounces
breadcrumbs		
dry	125	4½
soft	60	2
butter	250	8¾
cheese, grated cheddar	125	4½
flour		
cornflour	130	4¾
plain or self-raising	125	4½
wholemeal	135	4¾
fruit, mixed dried	160	5¾
honey	360	12¾
nuts	125	4½
rice		
brown uncooked	180	6¼
white uncooked	200	7
sugar		
castor	225	8
granulated	250	8¾
icing	175	6¼
moist brown	170	6
Farex cereal	75	2½

Microwaving for your baby

First, *never* attempt to sterilise any equipment for your baby in the microwave oven. Stick to traditional methods. Microwaving is not suitable for sterilisation as air bubbles are often trapped against surfaces and germs next to them are not destroyed.

Heating milk

The microwave oven is convenient to heat bottles of milk in, but extreme care must be taken if you do so. The reason is that the milk inside the bottle will heat up directly from the microwaves, while the plastic is warmed gradually by the milk. When you take the bottle out of the oven it is possible for the plastic to feel quite cool, but the milk inside could be hot enough to scald the baby.

To heat milk safely, follow these guidelines.

- Only heat refrigerated milk. Do not let milk stand to reach room temperature.
- Never try to heat less than 120 ml of milk.
- Only heat plastic bottles in the microwave oven, not glass.
- Remove the cap, lid and teat from the bottle before placing in the microwave.
- Use MEDIUM (50–60%) power. 120 ml will take about 40 seconds, 200 ml 1 minute 15 seconds, and 240 ml will take about 1 minute 25 seconds to heat. Adjust timing depending on the wattage of your oven.
- Replace teat assembly and mix the milk thoroughly by gentle shaking.
- Test the milk on your forearm. It should be cool to the touch, not warm. If it feels at all warm you should let the milk cool down before use.
- Never boil milk, as nutrients will be lost.

Introduction to food

Most babies are introduced to their first solid food at four–six months. Some eagerly accept solids, while others are more reluctant and spit the food out, or refuse to open their mouths. Don't rush your baby – if he or she doesn't want to try food yet wait for a week or two before offering it again.

Remember too that for the first few months of solid food milk will remain the most important part of baby's diet, and the new foods should be given in small amounts. By twelve months most babies should be eating a mixed diet of three meals a day, with between-meal snacks if necessary, and milk will play a lesser role, but should still be part of the diet every day.

When introducing solid foods it is important to try one at a time, rather than mixed together, and to give baby a few days to adjust to each food before trying a new one. If baby does not like any particular food, or shows an allergic reaction, don't persist with that food. You may be able to try it again at a later stage.

Rice cereal is often the first food given to babies, as it is easily digested. Commercial brands have added nutrients. When baby is eating rice cereal happily fruit and vegetable purées can be introduced, followed by fish, chicken and lean meat a few weeks later. If you are worried about possible allergies you should be careful when introducing wheat – for instance in bread, flour and many breakfast cereals – tomatoes, strawberries and citrus fruits. However, the vast majority of children are not sensitive to any food. Eggs should not be introduced before nine months, and then very carefully, as babies can be allergic to egg white.

Heating convenience baby foods

Although a variety of home-cooked foods is the best introduction to eating for your baby, there are times when commercial cans or jars of food are sensible choices for a rushed parent. They are particularly useful when on holiday, or visiting away from home.

To heat canned baby food in a microwave oven, empty contents of the can into a small microware bowl and heat for 15 seconds on HIGH (90–100%). Stir very well and test for temperature before feeding baby. Food in glass jars can be heated directly in the jars, *with the lid off*.

Freezer-to-highchair cooking

You can maximise the usefulness of your microwave by using it in combination with a freezer. First you can cook the food in convenient small amounts, quickly and economically; anything not eaten straight away can be frozen, and the microwave used to defrost and heat it as required. With just a little planning, you can have a ready supply of home-made baby food on hand in a matter of minutes.

The advantages of preparing baby food in the microwave are enormous. First, it is much more economical to make your own dishes than to buy an equivalent commercial product. You will then also have confidence that the meal contains no additives and is full of nutrients. When you need a meal, you can defrost and reheat one from the freezer as quickly as you could prepare a bought one.

Buy seasonal ingredients of good quality, cook some for baby and use the rest for the family. You can store cooked baby food in the refrigerator for two or three days. Use what you need and keep the rest chilled in small plastic containers set aside specially for baby's meals.

If you are going to freeze part of the recipe, you should do this as soon as the food is cold. A convenient way of freezing small portions is to use a sterilised ice-cube tray. The compartments hold about 20 g of cooked food. Once the food has frozen, transfer the cubes to microwave-safe freezer bags, labelled and dated clearly. When you want to use them, remove the number of cubes you require, resealing the bag with the remainder of the cubes. Do not let cubes begin to thaw if you are returning them to the freezer.

Here are some guidelines to the maximum time you should keep precooked recipes for baby in the freezer.

1 week Fish; liver.
2 months Mixed meat and vegetable purées; cheese dishes; white sauces.
3 months Beef, lamb, veal and poultry; soups; stocks.
6 months Fruit; juice; cakes.

Nutrition for babies and toddlers

Many nutrients are vital for proper growth and development, but fortunately there are plenty of different, delicious ways for even the fussiest eater to meet the daily dietary requirements. Here are some of the most important nutrients for your growing child.

Protein

For their size, children need proportionately more protein than adults. Protein is essential for normal growth. Breast and formula milk contain high-quality protein – that is, protein containing all the amino acids needed by the body. Many other foods contain high-quality protein, in particular meat, poultry, fish and seafood, eggs and dairy products.

Rice, pasta, legumes (beans, peas and lentils), bread, cereals, nuts and seeds all contain varying amounts of protein, but they need to be combined together in meals to obtain high-quality protein.

Carbohydrate

Complex carbohydrate is essential for energy and should form the basis of a healthy diet. Foods rich in complex carbohydrate include rice, bread, pasta, cereals, fruit, legumes and starchy vegetables.

Fats

While a diet too high in fat can predispose us to diseases, everyone requires some fat in their diet, and children need more than adults. Breast and formula milks provide around 50 per cent of a baby's energy needs as fat. Until about four or five years old, around 35 per cent of the energy children require should come from fat. This should then reduce to 30 per cent until puberty, after which fat intake should be the same as an adult's – less than 25 per cent of energy needs.

Children should not be encouraged to eat large amounts of fried foods, biscuits, cakes and lollies, but they should eat more nutritious fat-containing foods, such as lean meat, chicken, fish, dairy foods and avocado, and small amounts of peanut butter, nuts (when older) and margarine.

Dietary fibre

Fibre is an important part of children's diets, helping to regularise bowel movements and control appetite. However, large amounts of fibre should not be introduced too early, and young children may tolerate the fibre from fruit, rice, oats and barley better than bran cereals and foods that contain whole grains. With a high-fibre diet it is important to drink plenty of water.

Salt

Young babies dislike the taste of salt, but develop a liking for it over a period of time. Too much salt can cause problems for babies under 12 months, as their kidneys cannot cope with large amounts of sodium. The salt present naturally in food is more than enough to meet children's needs, so avoid adding salt to food, even though it may taste bland to you.

Vitamins and minerals

Many vitamins and minerals are necessary for healthy growth. In a balanced diet these should all be present in sufficient amounts. Here are a few of the more important ones.

Vitamin A — Important for normal eyesight and growth; also increases resistance to infection.

Thiamin (Vitamin B1) — Helps the release of energy from food and the use of oxygen by the body.

Niacin (Vitamin B3) — Essential for a healthy skin, gut and mind.

Pyridoxine (Vitamin B6) — Essential for building protein in the body.

Vitamin B12 — Only found in animal products, it is needed to form red blood cells.

Folate	Works with Vitamin B12 to form red blood cells, and is also involved in the production of protein.
Vitamin C	Many roles, including building and maintenance of bones, teeth, gums and blood. Also helps with the absorption of iron.
Vitamin D	Helps our bodies absorb calcium and phosphorus to build strong bones. Vitamin D can be produced by our bodies when sunlight falls on the skin.
Vitamin E	Important for the growth and maintenance of tissues and membranes. It may also play a role in the prevention of cancer.
Vitamin K	Needed for the clotting of blood. Newborn babies are often given Vitamin K as breast milk is relatively low in this vitamin.
Iron	Essential for making red blood cells. As children grow, their iron requirements increase. At seven–eight months, the iron in breast milk will not be sufficient for a baby's needs, and other sources of iron such as baby cereal and green vegetables are essential. Lack of iron can affect the learning ability of children.
Zinc	Essential for healthy skin, normal growth and development, and healing of wounds.
Calcium and phosphorus	Essential for the formation and growth of bones and muscles. An adequate intake of both is vital throughout the growing years.
Magnesium	Also important in development of normal bone, and is involved in energy production.

RECIPES

Four to six months

At this age breast milk or formula milk should still contribute 100 per cent of an infant's nutritional requirements. Offer solid foods in small amounts only. By six months baby may be having solid food at three meals, *in addition to the usual breast or formula feeds.*

When introducing solids, try one food at a time, and give baby time to adjust to each food before trying a new one. For example, you might offer something like this.

Day	*Food*
1–4	Rice Purée
5–8	Carrot Purée
9–12	Banana Mash
13–16	Spinach Purée
17–20	Fruity Rice Purée

Sample meal plan for a six-month-old

Breakfast	Fruity Rice Purée (p. 29)
Lunch	Spinach Purée (p. 24)
Dinner	Apple Purée (p. 26)

Most of the dietary requirements will still be provided by the milk. The recipes in this book do, however, give a breakdown of the nutrients available in an average serve.

Recommended dietary intake of an average six-month baby

Energy	3640 kJ (865 kCal)
Protein	14.0 g
Carbohydrate	126 g or less
Fat	at least 34 g
Thiamin	0.4 mg
Riboflavin	0.5 mg
Niacin	8.0 mg
Vitamin C	25.0 mg
Calcium	500.0 mg
Iron	3.0 mg

RICE PURÉE *from 4 months*

Use as an introduction to cereals or, later, as a base for sweet or savoury dishes.

INGREDIENTS
1 tablespoon ground rice
1 cup water

METHOD
1. Mix rice and water well in a small microware container.
2. Cook on HIGH (90-100%) for 2 minutes, stirring occasionally.
3. Reduce power to MEDIUM (50–60%), cook for 2 minutes, stirring regularly.
4. Cool to room temperature or chill ready for use.

VARIATIONS
- Mix rice with formula or expressed milk.
- Mix with puréed apple or pear.

POINTER
- Ground white rice can be purchased in the flour section of a supermarket. Brown rice has to be ground using a food processor or blender.

NUTRIENTS
(Average per ½ cup)
Energy 120 kJ (29 kCal)

Protein	0.54 g
Fat	0.04 g
Carbohydrate	6.49 g
Thiamin	0.01 mg
Riboflavin	0.00 mg
Niacin	0.16 mg
Vitamin C	0.00 mg
Calcium	0.58 mg
Iron	0.06 mg

POTATO PURÉE *from 4 months*

The homely spud is versatile: there are many varieties to choose from, and they are inexpensive and convenient to store. The easy, nutritious way to cook them in your microwave is with the skin on.

INGREDIENTS
1 small (70 g) potato

METHOD
1. Pierce potato with a toothpick 2–3 times.
2. Place off the centre of the turntable and microwave on HIGH (90-100%) for 2 minutes, turning over once.
3. Stand until cool. Cut in half and scoop out purée.

VARIATIONS
- **To make larger quantities** and freeze portions, use a large potato (a 200 g Pontiac, for example). Pierce in the same way, and cook on HIGH (90–100%) for 4 minutes, turning once. Let cool and mash purée. 2 medium potatoes will take 6 minutes, 3 potatoes 8 minutes.
- At six months you can add chicken stock when mashing, for a change of flavour.

FREEZING
- 200 g potato purée will fill 6 ice-cube cavities. Freeze until solid. Transfer to microwave-safe plastic bags, label and date and return to freezer.
- DEFROST (30-35%) 1 cube in microware bowl for 1 minute.

POINTER
- Potatoes are bland, and contain substantial amounts of Vitamin C, minerals and fibre, so are one of the first foods you can try baby with.

NUTRIENTS
(Average per serve)
Energy 184 kJ (44 kCal)

Protein	1.75 g
Fat	0.07 g
Carbohydrate	8.96 g
Thiamin	0.06 mg
Riboflavin	0.01 mg
Niacin	0.63 mg
Vitamin C	14.70 mg
Calcium	2.80 mg
Iron	0.35 mg

BUTTERNUT PUMPKIN PURÉE

from 4–4½ months

Pumpkin is smooth-textured and easy to peel using a microwave oven. Pear-shaped butternut is one of the first tastes baby can try. Sweet and easy to digest, it mixes well with other vegetables and even fruit.

INGREDIENT

1 small whole pumpkin (about 500 g), unpeeled

METHOD

1. Pierce the pumpkin's skin half a dozen times with a bamboo skewer, elevate on a roasting rack (or small saucer) and place off the centre of the turntable.
2. Microwave on HIGH (90-100%) for 8–10 minutes, turning over once.
3. Stand until cool.
4. Cut in half, remove seeds and scrape puréed pumpkin from the skin.
5. Take one serve for baby, mashed well, and use the rest for the family, seasoned and garnished with fresh herbs. Alternatively freeze excess.

VARIATIONS

- To cook only one portion, wrap a 100 g piece of pumpkin, skin on, in microwave-safe plastic wrap. Place off the centre of the turntable and microwave on HIGH (90–100%) for 2–3 minutes. Stand until cool. Remove skin and mash well.
- Mix pumpkin purée with potato or spinach purée, or banana mash.

FREEZING

- Freeze in ice-cube tray until solid. Transfer to microwave-safe plastic bags, label and date and return to freezer.
- DEFROST (30-35%) 1 cube in microwave bowl for 1 minute.

POINTER

- Heat a raw pumpkin in your microwave oven on HIGH (90–100%) for 2–3 minutes to soften and make easy to chop. Pierce skin first.

NUTRIENTS

(Average per serve of 100 g)
Energy 194 kJ (46 kCal)

Protein	2.30 g
Fat	0.70 g
Carbohydrate	7.70 g
Thiamin	0.07 mg
Riboflavin	0.09 mg
Niacin	0.50 mg
Vitamin C	6.00 mg
Calcium	22.00 mg
Iron	0.40 mg

SQUASH OR ZUCCHINI PURÉE

from 4–4½ months

Bland inside the skin, these vegetable members of the gourd family can be offered to baby early on. Some babies find the skin bitter, so use it to cook in and then remove it.

INGREDIENT

1 medium squash or zucchini (about 70 g)

METHOD

1. Rinse squash or zucchini, pierce with a toothpick several times and place off the centre of the turntable.
2. Microwave on HIGH (90–100%) for 1½ minutes.
3. Stand until cool, then split in half and remove purée.

VARIATIONS

- **For a larger zucchini** (about 150 g), microwave on HIGH for 2–3 minutes.
- Mix purée with puréed carrot or potato.

FREEZING

- Fills 3 ice-cube cavities. Freeze until solid. Transfer to microwave-safe plastic bags, label and date and return to freezer.
- DEFROST (30-35%) 1 cube in microware bowl for 1 minute.

POINTER

- Zucchini is a moist vegetable, consisting of 94.6 per cent water, so it needs rinse water only when cooking in the microwave oven.

NUTRIENTS

(Average per serve)
Energy 82 kJ (20 kCal)

Protein	2.10 g
Fat	0.14 g
Carbohydrate	2.52 g
Thiamin	0.02 mg
Riboflavin	0.04 mg
Niacin	0.28 mg
Vitamin C	12.60 mg
Calcium	4.20 mg
Iron	0.21 mg

SPINACH PURÉE *from 4–4½ months*

Green, leafy vegetables are rich in iron and fresh or frozen spinach is a good source. As baby approaches 6 months, breast milk no longer supplies enough iron, and solids must provide it to ensure healthy blood and strong muscles.

INGREDIENT

200 g spinach leaves, well washed

METHOD

1. Put spinach in a medium-size microware container, cover and place off the centre of the turntable. Microwave on HIGH (90–100%) for 2½ minutes. Stand to cool, then purée in a blender or push through a fine sieve. Purée should make 4 baby serves.
2. Mix 1 purée serving with breast milk or formula until moist.

VARIATIONS

- For older children or adults, unused spinach can be made into a cream of spinach soup by placing leaves in a 4-cup microware jug and adding 2 cups milk, 1 teaspoon butter and a pinch of nutmeg. Partially cover the jug and microwave on HIGH (90–100%) for 5–6 minutes, stirring several times. Purée soup in the blender.
- **To make individual serve,** use 50 g spinach leaves and microwave on HIGH (90–100%) for 1½ minutes. Cool, then purée.

FREEZING

- Fills 4 ice-cube cavities with spinach purée. Freeze until solid. Transfer to microwave-safe plastic bags, label and date and return to freezer.
- DEFROST (30-35%) 1 cube in microware bowl for 1 minute.

POINTER

- 250 g finely chopped frozen spinach defrosts quickly in the microwave for purée, if you are in a hurry. Simply place in a small microware container, cover and thaw on HIGH (90–100%) for 5 minutes. Drain off excess fluid and remove a serve for baby.

NUTRIENTS

(Average per serve)

Energy 39 kJ (9 kCal)

Protein	1.50 g
Fat	0.20 g
Carbohydrate	0.40 g
Thiamin	0.03 mg
Riboflavin	0.08 mg
Niacin	0.20 mg
Vitamin C	8.00 mg
Calcium	25.00 mg
Iron	1.50 mg

CARROT PURÉE *from 4½ months*

Carrots are a great source of Vitamin A, important for good eyesight. Let baby discover the true taste of tender carrots by cooking them in their skins, or in minimal water, to enhance the flavour. Try offering puréed carrots after potato and pumpkin and later as a finger food.

INGREDIENT
1 medium (100 g) carrot

METHOD
1. Pierce carrot several times.
2. Place carrot on a piece of white paper towel on the turntable, with the thicker section of the carrot towards the outer edge.
3. Microwave on HIGH (90–100%) for 2–3 minutes, turning over once.
4. Stand to cool, halve lengthways and scrape out the flesh with a knife. Sieve or mash well.

VARIATIONS
- Initially mix carrot purée with expressed breast milk or formula. From six months, add some lamb or chicken stock.
- **To make a larger amount**, peel and slice 6 medium carrots (500 g) thinly. Put in medium container with 2 tablespoons water. Cover and place towards the edge of the turntable. Cook on HIGH (90–100%) for 10–11 minutes. Blend well. Makes 2 cups.
- Turn purée into a soup for older children by placing 1 cup carrot purée together with 1 cup chicken stock, 1 cup milk and a pinch of mace. Cook in a 4-cup jug, partially covered with microwave-safe plastic wrap, on HIGH (90–100%) for 5–6 minutes, stirring several times. Serve with finely chopped parsley.

FREEZING
- Freeze in ice-cube trays until solid. Transfer to microwave-safe plastic bags, label and date and return to freezer.
- DEFROST (30-35%) 1 cube in microware bowl for 1 minute.

POINTER
- When adding carrot to casseroles, meat loaves and baby burgers grate it instead of chopping it. This will ensure it cooks completely, in the shorter cooking time of the microwave.

NUTRIENTS
(Average per serve)
Energy 112 kJ (27 kCal)

Protein	0.90 g
Fat	0.10 g
Carbohydrate	5.60 g
Thiamin	0.07 mg
Riboflavin	0.04 mg
Niacin	0.70 mg
Vitamin C	4.00 mg
Calcium	29.00 mg
Iron	0.30 mg

APPLE PURÉE *from 4 months*

Always available and inexpensive, apples make a fine first food for baby.

INGREDIENT

1 large Jonathan or Delicious apple, about 170 g

METHOD

1. Core apply carefully, ensuring all pips are removed. Pierce the skin several times with a toothpick.
2. Place apple in microware bowl off the centre of the turntable and microwave on HIGH (90–100%) for 3½ minutes.
3. Allow to stand until cool enough to open skin and scoop out the purée.

VARIATION

- Mix equal amounts of apple purée together with mashed banana or sweet potato purée. Moisten with a little apple juice.

FREEZING

- Fills 3 ice-cube cavities. Freeze until solid. Transfer to microwave-safe plastic bags, label and date and return to freezer.
- DEFROST (30-35%) for 1 minute in microware bowl.

POINTER

- For maximum nutrition and convenience, microwave apples with skin on.

NUTRIENTS
(Average per serve)
Energy 231 kJ (55 kCal)

Protein	0.51 g
Fat	0.00 g
Carbohydrate	13.94 g
Thiamin	0.05 mg
Riboflavin	0.03 mg
Niacin	0.17 mg
Vitamin C	20.40 mg
Calcium	5.10 mg
Iron	0.51 mg

PEAR PURÉE *from 4 months*

One of the earliest fruits to offer your baby, along with apple. Cooking time will vary depending on the ripeness of the pears.

INGREDIENT

1 ripe, firm pear, about 200 g

METHOD

1. Pierce skin of pear several times.
2. Place pear on edge of turntable, ensuring the thickest part of the pear is towards the outer edge.
3. Microwave on HIGH (90–100%) for 2½–3 minutes. Stand to cool.
4. Cut in half, remove core and pips, then scoop out purée.
5. Use amount required and refrigerate the balance.

VARIATIONS

- Initially mix purée with rice cereal. For older babies, mix with mashed bananas, apple purée or stewed rhubarb.
- **To make a larger amount** peel and core 4 ripe pears (about 500 g). Slice thinly, put in medium-size container, cover and place at edge of turntable. Cook on HIGH (90–100%) for 5–6 minutes. Stand for 2–3 minutes to cool, then blend. Makes 1¼ cups (300 ml).

FREEZING

- Freeze until solid in ice-cube trays. Transfer to microwave-safe plastic bags, label and date and return to freezer.
- DEFROST (30-35%) 1 cube in microware bowl for 1 minute.

POINTERS

- Frozen purée should not be completely defrosted by microwave, but still be cold and firm for the best flavour and texture.
- If defrosting in microwave-safe plastic pouches, gently squeeze pouch from time to time to distribute the fruit.

NUTRIENTS

(Average per serve)

Energy 396 kJ (95 kCal)

Protein	0.60 g
Fat	0.00 g
Carbohydrate	23.60 g
Thiamin	0.04 mg
Riboflavin	0.06 mg
Niacin	0.20 mg
Vitamin C	12.00 mg
Calcium	12.00 mg
Iron	0.40 mg

BANANA MASH *from 4 months*

A two-minute wonder when a ripe, speckled fruit is not readily available.

INGREDIENT

1 firm banana

METHOD

1. Place unpeeled banana off the centre of the turntable and microwave on LOW (30–40%) for 1 minute.
2. Turn fruit over and microwave on LOW (30–40%) for a further 1 minute.
3. Stand for 1 minute before peeling and mashing.

FREEZING

- For an easy snack for children twelve months or older mix a banana with yoghurt and freeze in ice blocks until solid. Transfer to microwave-safe plastic bags, label and date and return to freezer.
- DEFROST (30-35%) 1 cube in a microware bowl for 1 minute.

POINTERS

- Overcooking a banana results in the fruit blackening.
- A quick snack for an older child can be made by heating a firm banana in its skin on HIGH (90-100%) for 45-60 seconds and serving with home-made custard (p. 152) or ice cream.

NUTRIENTS
(Average per serve)
Energy 501 kJ (120 kCal)

Nutrient	Amount
Protein	2.38 g
Fat	0.14 g
Carbohydrate	27.86 g
Thiamin	0.07 mg
Riboflavin	0.15 mg
Niacin	0.56 mg
Vitamin C	16.80 mg
Calcium	7.00 mg
Iron	0.70 mg

FRUITY RICE PURÉE

from 4–5 months

INGREDIENTS

½ cup apple juice, chilled
2 teaspoons ground rice

METHOD

1. Mix apple juice and ground rice together in a small microware container.
2. Cook on HIGH (90–100%) for 3 minutes, stirring regularly.
3. Cool and serve at room temperature.

VARIATION

- Pear juice can be used in place of apple juice.

POINTER

- Use rice flour instead of ground rice for a smoother texture.

NUTRIENTS
(Average per serve)
Energy 298 kJ (71 kCal)

Protein	0.67 g
Fat	0.04 g
Carbohydrate	17.11 g
Thiamin	0.01 mg
Riboflavin	0.01 mg
Niacin	0.29 mg
Vitamin C	38.75 mg
Calcium	5.57 mg
Iron	0.31 mg

APRICOTS AU NATUREL

from 5–6 months

After you have tried baby on apple and pear, introduce baby to the colourful apricot, which provides Vitamin A and potassium. Makes about 5–6 serves.

INGREDIENT

500 g apricots

METHOD

1. Place apricots around edge of a large microware container.
2. Microwave on HIGH (90–100%) for about 3 minutes.
3. Allow to cool, halve and stone. Remove fruit from skins.

VARIATION

- Mix with other fruits that your baby likes such as apples or pears.

POINTERS

- Ripe apricots done this way will cook enough to purée. Firm apricots stew, but still hold their shape.
- Timing varies with the ripeness of the fruit.
- Apricots are high in sugar and thus should not be overcooked as they will blacken during standing time.

NUTRIENTS
(Average per serve of 100 g)
Energy 156 kJ (37 kCal)

Nutrient	Amount
Protein	0.80 g
Fat	0.10 g
Carbohydrate	7.40 g
Thiamin	0.03 mg
Riboflavin	0.04 mg
Niacin	1.50 mg
Vitamin C	12.00 mg
Calcium	16.00 mg
Iron	0.30 mg

APPLE JUICE *from 4 months*

Makes about 3 cups.

INGREDIENTS

4 medium Jonathan apples
4 cups hot water

METHOD

1. Rinse fruit. Chop into 4-cm cubes, leaving skin on and cores intact.
2. Place in a large microware container, pour over hot water, cover and microwave on HIGH (90–100%) in the centre of the turntable for 12–15 minutes.
3. Strain and pour into containers.

VARIATION

- Firm pears may be used in place of apples.

FREEZING

- Freeze in well-washed 300 ml milk cartons until required.
- DEFROST (30-35%) for 5 minutes.

POINTERS

- Cooking time is relatively long because of the amount of liquid in the recipe. Using hot liquid will speed up the cooking time when making juices, soups and stocks.
- Delicious apples may be substituted for Jonathans. Use Granny Smith apples for older children.

NUTRIENTS
(Average per ½ cup)
Energy 208 kJ (50 kCal)

Nutrient	Amount
Protein	0.30 g
Fat	0.00 g
Carbohydrate	12.30 g
Thiamin	0.02 mg
Riboflavin	0.01 mg
Niacin	0.10 mg
Vitamin C	5.00 mg
Calcium	4.00 mg
Iron	0.20 mg

CHRISTOPHER'S CAMOMILE TEA SOOTHER

from 5 months

Camomile is a healing plant of great antiquity; it makes a soothing tea for stomach upsets and indigestion.

INGREDIENTS

1 teaspoon camomile tea leaves
300 ml water

METHOD

1. Bring water to boil in a 4-cup ovenable glass jug on HIGH (90–100%) for 2–3 minutes.
2. Lightly sprinkle the top with camomile tea leaves.
3. Simmer on DEFROST (30–35%) for 5 minutes, then let stand for 3 minutes to infuse.
4. Strain through a fine sieve and pour into a sterilised bottle.
5. Serve to baby at body temperature.

POINTER

- You can buy camomile tea bags in the health food section of any supermarket, or alternatively health food shops stock camomile tea in bulk for approximately $3.00 per kilo.

Seven to twelve months

During these months solid food will play an increasing part in the diet of your baby, and by one year he or she should be eating three meals a day, with snacks mid-morning and mid-afternoon. Meat, fish and eggs will be introduced into baby's food. Milk will also be important, but when you are offering baby a full meal give the milk after rather than before, so that baby has some appetite for the solids. Cow's milk can be introduced in dishes from six months but should not become the primary source of milk until after twelve months. Always offer whole cow's milk to children, as reduced fat milk loses valuable vitamins with its cream.

Teeth will also be appearing over these months – some babies like to chew on finger food when teething, while others seem to lose their appetite for a day or two and prefer milk.

Sample meal plan for a twelve-month-old

Breakfast	Orange Juice (p. 60), Fruity Weetbix (p. 36)
Snack	Choc-nana Smoothie (p. 59)
Lunch	Scrambled Eggs (p. 35), 1 slice wholemeal bread
Snack	Stewed Apple (p. 54), 1 cup milk
Dinner	Cream of Vegetable Soup (p. 41), Poached Fish with White Sauce (p. 43), Fresh Asparagus (p. 53)
Snack	Yoghurt Jelly (p. 57)

Recommended dietary intake of an average twelve-month-old

Energy	5200 kJ (1238 kCal)
Protein	16.0 g
Carbohydrate	185 g or less
Fat	at least 48 g
Thiamin	0.5 mg
Riboflavin	0.8 mg
Niacin	8.3 mg
Vitamin C	30.0 mg
Calcium	700.0 mg
Iron	6.0 mg

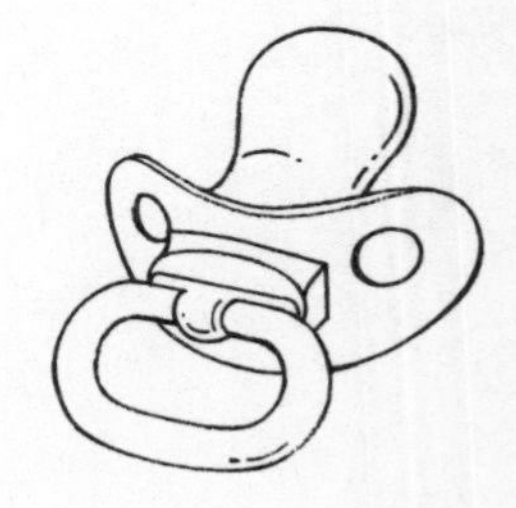

OAT PORRIDGE *from 7–8 months*

Porridge is an easy way of introducing oats into your baby's diet. Being part of the cereal and bread food group, oats contain carbohydrates that supply energy and are a good source of Vitamin B.

INGREDIENTS

¼ cup instant oats
½ cup warm water

METHOD

1. Place oats and water in a medium microwave bowl and cook on HIGH (90–100%) for 1½ minutes.
2. Stir well. Stand for 1 minute.
3. Mix with a little milk or formula to serve.

VARIATIONS

- Slice ¼ banana into the oats and cook as above.
- Mix uncooked oats with warm apple juice instead of water.
- Stir in 2 teaspoons sultanas before standing (for children over nine months).

POINTERS

- Rolled oats can be ground in a blender and used instead of instant oats, as they cook faster in the microwave.
- Porridge tends to boil over, so use a medium size container for a single serve.

NUTRIENTS
(Average per serve)
Energy 367 kJ (88 kCal)

Nutrient	Amount
Protein	2.54 g
Fat	2.02 g
Carbohydrate	14.68 g
Thiamin	0.13 mg
Riboflavin	0.03 mg
Niacin	0.24 mg
Vitamin C	0.00 mg
Calcium	10.69 mg
Iron	0.88 mg

SCRAMBLED EGGS

from 12 months

Eggs are an easily digested form of high-quality protein. A great recipe for growing children. The golden rule when cooking eggs in the microwave oven is always to undercook so they do not toughen.

INGREDIENTS

1 egg
1 tablespoon milk

METHOD

1. Beat egg well with a fork in a small microware bowl. Add milk and stir well.
2. Place on the edge of the turntable and microwave on HIGH (90–100%) for 30–40 seconds, stirring a couple of times during cooking.
3. Serve with toast.

VARIATION

- Stir in a few leftover cooked peas for colour.

POINTER

- Cook with eggs that are at room temperature for even results.

NUTRIENTS
(Average per serve)
Energy 343 kJ (82 kCal)

Nutrient	Amount
Protein	6.61 g
Fat	5.39 g
Carbohydrate	1.86 g
Thiamin	0.04 mg
Riboflavin	0.22 mg
Niacin	0.16 mg
Vitamin C	1.12 mg
Calcium	36.09 mg
Iron	1.02 mg

FRUITY WEETBIX

from 12 months

These are very popular with babies and easy for mothers.

INGREDIENTS
½ cup apple juice
1 Weetbix

METHOD
1. Warm apple juice in a small microware bowl on HIGH (90–100%) for 45 seconds.
2. Add Weetbix and allow to soften, then mash.

VARIATION
Use pear juice in place of apple juice.

NUTRIENTS
(Average per serve)
Energy 403 kJ (96 kCal)

Protein	2.01 g
Fat	0.39 g
Carbohydrate	21.20 g
Thiamin	0.16 mg
Riboflavin	0.26 mg
Niacin	2.32 mg
Vitamin C	38.75 mg
Calcium	10.10 mg
Iron	1.71 mg

POACHED EGGS *from 12 months*

Eggs are versatile and a poached egg makes a nutritious hot meal or a tasty sandwich spread.

INGREDIENT

1 large egg at room temperature

METHOD

1. Crack egg into a small microware bowl. Pierce the yolk. Cover with microwave-safe plastic wrap and place off the centre of the turntable.
2. Microwave on MEDIUM (50–60%) for 30–45 seconds. Stand for 1 minute.
3. Serve on toast or with toast fingers.

VARIATION

- Mash egg with a little milk, mayonnaise, tomato sauce or grated cheddar cheese.

POINTERS

- Eggs cook best in the microwave oven from room temperature in an ovenable glass custard cup, covered.
- Eggs mash more easily if not hard cooked. Mashed eggs can be left to cool for sandwiches.

NUTRIENTS

(Average per serve)

Energy 295 kJ (70 kCal)

Nutrient	Amount
Protein	5.78 g
Fat	5.26 g
Carbohydrate	0.14 g
Thiamin	0.04 mg
Riboflavin	0.14 mg
Niacin	0.09 mg
Vitamin C	0.00 mg
Calcium	24.91 mg
Iron	0.94 mg

CHICKEN STOCK *from 7 months*

Everyone's heard of the comforting benefits of chicken soup. A home-made stock acts as its base, as well as being a useful addition to purées, casseroles and sauces. It is better for babies and toddlers than commercial stock, which is often high in salt, as infants' kidneys cannot cope with large amounts of salt. Makes approximately 5 cups.

INGREDIENTS

1 boiling chicken (about 1.2 kg)
1 large onion (optional), quartered
2 sticks celery, leaves included, chopped in 4-cm pieces
1 large carrot, cut into rounds
sprig of fresh parsley
6 cups hot water

METHOD

1. Cut the chicken into 6 portions and remove skin from each piece.
2. Place chicken and vegetables in the base of a large microware container. Pour over hot water. Cover container.
3. Place in the centre of the turntable and microwave on HIGH (90–100%) for 15 minutes to bring to the boil.
4. Reduce power to DEFROST (30–35%) and microwave for 45 minutes.
5. Stand to cool, then place in refrigerator to chill.
6. Skim fat from top and strain stock through a fine sieve.
7. Store in refrigerator or freeze.

FREEZING

- Pour into ice-cube trays or into well-washed milk cartons of 300 ml or 600 ml sizes. Freeze until solid. Transfer cubes to microwave-safe plastic bags, label and date and return to freezer.
- DEFROST (30-35%) 1 cube in a microware bowl for 1 minute. For 300 ml carton, microwave on HIGH (90–100%) for 5 minutes. For 600 ml carton, microwave on HIGH (90–100%) for 7 minutes.

NUTRIENTS

(Average per ½ cup)
Energy 334 kJ (80 kCal)

Nutrient	Amount
Protein	10.61 g
Fat	3.94 g
Carbohydrate	0.45 g
Thiamin	0.03 mg
Riboflavin	0.11 mg
Niacin	1.83 mg
Vitamin C	0.58 mg
Calcium	9.74 mg
Iron	0.48 mg

LAMB STOCK *from 7 months*

Add this stock to prepared vegetables for baby from six months and introduce the meat into baby's diet at seven–eight months. This recipe makes 1 litre.

INGREDIENTS

1 lamb shank
1 carrot (about 125 g)
1 stick celery
4 cups water

METHOD

1. Place all ingredients in a large microware container.
2. Cover and microwave on HIGH (90–100%) for 5 minutes.
3. Reduce power to LOW (30–40%) and cook for a further 30 minutes, covered.
4. Allow to cool. Strain stock and chill. Remove fat from surface.

VARIATION

- Use the meat from the cooked lamb shank to make a fricassee – a dish of meat and white sauce (see p. 145) – for older children.

FREEZING

- Pour into ice-cube trays or into well-washed 300 ml milk cartons, label and date. Freeze until solid. Transfer cubes to microwave-safe plastic bags, label and date and return to freezer.
- DEFROST (30-35%) 1 cube in a microware bowl for 1 minute. For 300 ml carton, microwave on HIGH (90-100%) for 5 minutes to defrost.

POINTER

- Several slices of well-cooked lean lamb from the family roast can be used to make baby a purée. Blend with a little stock until a smooth texture.

NUTRIENTS
(Average per ½ cup)
Energy 99 kJ (24 kCal)

Nutrient	Amount
Protein	4.45 g
Fat	0.36 g
Carbohydrate	0.60 g
Thiamin	0.02 mg
Riboflavin	0.04 mg
Niacin	0.79 mg
Vitamin C	0.51 mg
Calcium	6.60 mg
Iron	0.38 mg

BEEF STOCK *from 7 months*

Harder to digest than white meats, introduce beef into baby's diet in the form of stock. Once you have established that baby does not react to beef, purée a little of the meat itself and mix it with vegetables.

INGREDIENTS
250 g osso bucco (beef shank)
1 litre warm water
1 medium carrot
2 sticks celery

METHOD
1. Trim fat from meat. Place in a large microware container with water. Cover with lid and cook on HIGH (90–100%) for 5 minutes.
2. Peel carrot. Chop carrot and celery into 3-cm pieces. Add to container, cover and microwave on LOW (30–40%) for 30 minutes.
3. Strain stock, chill, then skim off fat. Store in a sealed container in the refrigerator.

VARIATIONS
- Meat is nutritionally excellent. When cooking a family roast, keep a few well-cooked slices and purée them with the beef stock for baby.
- 1 small onion can be added to ingredients for children over ten months.

FREEZING
- Pour into ice-cube cavities or well-washed 300 ml milk cartons, label and date. Freeze until solid. Transfer cubes to microwave-safe plastic bags, label and date and return to freezer.
- DEFROST (30-35%) 1 cube in a microware bowl for 1 minute. For 300 ml carton, microwave on HIGH (90–100%) for 5 minutes to defrost.

POINTERS
- Using warm water allows the stock to come to the boil more quickly.
- Make sure meat used for stock is lean or trimmed of fat.

NUTRIENTS
(Average per 100 ml)
Energy 80 kJ (19 kCal)

Nutrient	Amount
Protein	3.88 g
Fat	0.09 g
Carbohydrate	0.66 g
Thiamin	0.02 mg
Riboflavin	0.06 mg
Niacin	0.84 mg
Vitamin C	0.63 mg
Calcium	8.96 mg
Iron	0.30 mg

CREAM OF VEGETABLE SOUP

from 8 months

Use vegetables in season for this soup, which can be made in minutes in the microwave. Purée chosen vegetable following suitable recipe on pp. 21–5. You can use a mixture of purées.

INGREDIENTS

1/4 cup Chicken Stock (p. 38)
1/3 cup vegetable purée
1/4 cup milk (expressed or formula)

METHOD

[1] Blend stock and vegetable purée together. Microwave on HIGH (90–100%) for 1 minute.

[2] Add milk, blend well and serve.

VARIATION

- Beef, lamb or Vegemite stock can be used in place of chicken stock.

NUTRIENTS
(Average per serve)
Energy 425 kJ (102 kCal)

Protein	9.27 g
Fat	4.31 g
Carbohydrate	6.44 g
Thiamin	0.07 mg
Riboflavin	0.17 mg
Niacin	1.98 mg
Vitamin C	10.82 mg
Calcium	67.05 mg
Iron	1.33 mg

SPEEDY VEGEMITE STOCK

from 9 months

High in the B vitamins and salt, Vegemite should not be given to young babies but introduced thinly spread on toast at around nine months. This speedy stock is handy for cold-weather casseroles.

INGREDIENTS

½ teaspoon Vegemite
200 ml hot water

METHOD

1. Put water into a 500 ml ovenable glass jug.
2. Set jug off the centre of the turntable and microwave on HIGH (90–100%) for 2 minutes.
3. Dissolve Vegemite in the boiling water and mix well.
4. Store covered in the refrigerator.

VARIATION

■ Add warm Vegemite stock to cover mixed vegetable casseroles. Casserole vegetables may be mashed when cooked or cut into smaller pieces.

POINTER

■ To make your own rusks to spread with Vegemite, cut the crusts off 3 slices of white or brown bread. Place on plain paper towel and microwave on HIGH (90–100%) for 2–3 minutes, turning over once. Store in an airtight container for finger food.

NUTRIENTS
(Average per ½ cup)
Energy 11 kJ (3 kCal)

Nutrient	Amount
Protein	0.45 g
Fat	0.00 g
Carbohydrate	0.23 g
Thiamin	0.18 mg
Riboflavin	0.25 mg
Niacin	1.72 mg
Vitamin C	0.00 mg
Calcium	0.78 mg
Iron	0.11 mg

POACHED FISH WITH WHITE SAUCE *from 7–8 months*

Fish is easily digestible and contains high-quality protein essential for growth. This recipe is an easy way of starting baby on fresh fish. Remember, if fish smells fishy, it is stale. This recipe makes approximately ⅔ cup.

INGREDIENTS

100 g flake fillet
⅓ cup milk (expressed or formula)
1 stalk parsley (optional)
1 tablespoon Farex cereal

METHOD

1. Place fish, milk and parsley in a small microware container and cook on HIGH (90–100%) for 2 minutes, turning fish once during cooking.
2. Remove fish and parsley. Add Farex to milk, stir to thicken.
3. Mash fish, or purée well for younger infants. Mix fish into white sauce.

VARIATION

- For older children, use a cheesy white sauce over whole fish or top white sauce with finely chopped parsley.
- For larger quantities, cook 500 g fish for 4–5 minutes on HIGH (90–100%).

FREEZING

- Fills 10 ice-cube compartments. Freeze until solid. Transfer to microwave-safe plastic bags, label and date and return to freezer.
- DEFROST (30-35%) for 1 minute per cube.

POINTER

- Do not overcook fish in your microwave oven or it will be tough and tasteless. It should be opaque at the end of cooking time.

NUTRIENTS
(Average per serve)
Energy 959 kJ (229 kCal)

Nutrient	Amount
Protein	33.53 g
Fat	2.86 g
Carbohydrate	17.33 g
Thiamin	0.34 mg
Riboflavin	0.42 mg
Niacin	13.13 mg
Vitamin C	5.15 mg
Calcium	204.14 mg
Iron	8.82 mg

BEEF AND VEGETABLE PURÉE

from 7 months

This is an easy way of introducing beef when first serving it to baby. It makes about 1½ cups.

INGREDIENTS

beef and vegetables strained from Beef Stock (p. 40)
⅓ cup Beef Stock (p. 40)

METHOD

1. Using the strained meat and vegetables from the beef stock, remove the bones.
2. Purée with stock.

VARIATIONS

- Dilute with extra stock to make a soup.
- Follow this recipe using the meat and vegetables from the Lamb Stock (p. 39).

FREEZING

- Fills 6 ice-cube cavities. Freeze until solid. Transfer to microwave-safe plastic bags, label and date and return to freezer.
- DEFROST (30-35%) 1 cube in a microware bowl for 1 minute.

NUTRIENTS
(Average per ½ cup)
Energy 232 kJ (58 kCal)

Protein	11.65 g
Fat	0.26 g
Carbohydrate	1.98 g
Thiamin	0.06 mg
Riboflavin	0.18 mg
Niacin	2.53 mg
Vitamin C	1.89 mg
Calcium	26.89 mg
Iron	0.91 mg

JUST CHICKEN *from 10 months*

Chicken cooks especially well in the microwave oven and forms the base of many soups, casseroles and light meals. Cooked this way, it can be used immediately or finished off on a barbecue on hot nights.

INGREDIENT
100 g chicken fillet, skinless

METHOD
1. Place fillet in a small microwave container or lid. Fold point of fillet under to make an even shape. Pierce fillet in several places.
2. Microwave on MEDIUM-HIGH (70–80%) for 1½–1¾ minutes, turning once during cooking.
3. Stand for 2 minutes.

VARIATION
- Chop and serve with a little White Sauce (p. 145).

FREEZING
- Wrap fillet in microwave-safe plastic wrap and freeze.
- DEFROST (30-35%) for 2 minutes. Stand at room temperature for 2 minutes.

POINTER
- Always pierce chicken before cooking in the microwave oven to allow steam to escape and prevent popping.

NUTRIENTS
(Average per serve)
Energy 660 kJ (158 kCal)

Protein	28.40 g
Fat	4.80 g
Carbohydrate	0.00 g
Thiamin	0.06 mg
Riboflavin	0.12 mg
Niacin	8.70 mg
Vitamin C	0.00 mg
Calcium	11.00 mg
Iron	0.60 mg

BRAINS IN WHITE SAUCE

from 10 months

Prepared in a light white sauce, brains provide a nutritious and economical meal for babies. Like other offal, brains are packed with minerals and vitamins – calcium, vitamins A and C, and B vitamins niacin, thiamin and riboflavin – as well as protein. This recipe makes 4 serves.

INGREDIENTS

1 set of brains (lamb or calf)
2–3 tablespoons White Sauce (p. 145)
1 teaspoon finely chopped fresh parsley

METHOD

1. Soak brains for several hours in water, then remove skin, all membranes and dark spots. It is important to prepare brains thoroughly. Rinse well.
2. Chop into 2-cm cubes and place in a small microware bowl. Cover.
3. Microwave on MEDIUM (50–60%) for 1½ minutes. Stir.
4. Microwave on MEDIUM (50–60%) for a further 1½ minutes. Stand for 2 minutes.
5. Stir in white sauce and parsley.
6. Purée for smaller babies or mash for older babies.

VARIATION

- Blend cooked brains with milk, formula or chicken stock.

POINTER

- Uncooked brains freeze well and are easier to clean when partially frozen.

NUTRIENTS
(Average per serve)
Energy 285 kJ (68 kCal)

Nutrient	Amount
Protein	3.86 g
Fat	5.05 g
Carbohydrate	1.99 g
Thiamin	0.05 mg
Riboflavin	0.14 mg
Niacin	1.15 mg
Vitamin C	3.20 mg
Calcium	40.80 mg
Iron	0.44 mg

KIDNEY VEGETABLE PURÉE

from 10 months

If your family enjoys offal, try baby on some combined with vegetables and a pouring sauce. This recipe makes about 5 baby's portions.

INGREDIENTS
2 lamb's kidneys
100 g puréed carrot
2 tablespoons White Sauce (p. 145)

METHOD
1. Halve, clean and soak kidneys for 10 minutes in 1 cup water and ½ teaspoon salt.
2. Drain kidneys and dice.
3. Microwave in a microware bowl on MEDIUM (50–60%) for 3–4 minutes, stirring once. Stand to cool.
4. Add carrot and white sauce. Blend until smooth.
5. Rewarm on MEDIUM (50–60%) for 1–2 minutes.
6. Remove a serve for baby.
7. Refrigerate remainder, covered, for other meals.

VARIATION
- Kidney vegetable purée can be mixed with rice cereal.

POINTER
- If you are going to cook kidneys whole, pierce them well before microwaving, to prevent popping.

NUTRIENTS
(Average per serve)
Energy 236 kJ (57 kCal)

Protein	4.49 g
Fat	3.13 g
Carbohydrate	2.70 g
Thiamin	0.14 mg
Riboflavin	0.46 mg
Niacin	1.60 mg
Vitamin C	4.23 mg
Calcium	39.12 mg
Iron	2.04 mg

BABY PÂTÉ *from 10 months*

Chicken livers are a handy food to have frozen as they defrost and cook excellently in the microwave oven. Chicken livers are also one of the most nutritious foods you can give to your baby and children – they are a rich source of protein, iron and zinc, and contain Vitamin B12, folate and pyridoxine. This recipe makes approximately 2 serves.

INGREDIENTS

1 medium potato
1 chicken liver
1 tablespoon Chicken Stock (p. 38)
a little milk

METHOD

1. Prick skin of potato well. Cook on HIGH (90–100%) for 3 minutes or until tender. Stand until cool, scoop out flesh and mash.
2. Chop liver. Place liver and stock in a small microware bowl. Cook on MEDIUM-HIGH (70–80%) for 1 minute, stirring occasionally.
3. Purée liver with stock and mashed potato. Adjust consistency with milk to suit infant.

VARIATION

Use a parsnip in place of the potato.

FREEZING

- Fills 4 ice-cube cavities. Freeze until solid. Transfer to microwave-safe plastic bags, label and date and return to freezer.
- DEFROST (30-35%) 1 cube for 1½ minutes. Stand for 1 minute.

POINTER

- To freeze uncooked chicken liver, chop it before freezing. 250 g is a useful amount to freeze per bag. To defrost, remove livers from the bag, place on a roasting rack (or upturned saucer) so the juices drain away and DEFROST (30-35%) for 5-8 minutes.

NUTRIENTS
(Average per serve)
Energy 304 kJ (73 kCal)

Protein	7.06 g
Fat	2.17 g
Carbohydrate	6.14 g
Thiamin	0.09 mg
Riboflavin	0.68 mg
Niacin	2.83 mg
Vitamin C	12.23 mg
Calcium	12.80 mg
Iron	2.63 mg

PARSNIP MASH *from 7 months*

Sweet-tasting parsnip can be cooked and used in place of potato for an interesting change.

INGREDIENT
1 medium parsnip (about 100 g)

METHOD
1. Pierce the skin of parsnip several times.
2. Place parsnip on the edge of the turntable, ensuring the thickest part of the parsnip is towards the outside.
3. Microwave on HIGH (90–100%) for 3 minutes, turning over once.
4. Stand to cool, then scrape out the flesh with a knife. Sieve or mash well.

VARIATIONS
- Mash with ½ teaspoon butter and finely chopped parsley.
- For older children, use as the base of Bubble and Squeak Slice (p. 78).
- **To make a larger quantity**, use 500 g parsnips. Peel and slice. Put in a medium container with ¼–½ cup water. Cover container and place towards edge of turntable. Cook on HIGH (90–100%) for 11–12 minutes. Drain and blend. This quantity makes about 1¼ cups.

FREEZING
- Freeze in ice-cube tray until solid. Transfer cubes to microwave-safe plastic bags, label and date and return to freezer.
- DEFROST (30-35%) 1 cube in microware bowl for 1 minute.

NUTRIENTS
(Average per serve)
Energy 208 kJ (50 kCal)

Nutrient	Amount
Protein	1.80 g
Fat	0.20 g
Carbohydrate	10.00 g
Thiamin	0.07 mg
Riboflavin	0.10 mg
Niacin	1.00 mg
Vitamin C	8.00 mg
Calcium	36.00 mg
Iron	0.30 mg

BEAN BONANZA *from 7 months*

INGREDIENT
30 g green beans, sliced lengthwise

METHOD
1. Place beans in a small microware bowl with ½ teaspoon water.
2. Cover and microwave on HIGH (90–100%) for 1½ minutes.
3. Stand, then purée to serve.

VARIATIONS
- Mix bean purée with potato or carrot purée.
- To cook 500 g of beans, place sliced beans in a cake-ring dish, or in a doughnut shape in a medium microware container, with ¼ cup of water. Cover and cook on HIGH (90–100%) for 10 minutes. Drain and purée.

FREEZING
- Freeze in ice-cube cavities until solid. Transfer to microwave-safe plastic bags, label and date and return to freezer.
- DEFROST (30-35%) 1 cube in a microware bowl for 1 minute.

POINTERS
- Slicing beans thinly ensures they cook quickly and evenly in your microwave.
- Minimal amounts of water and rapid microwaving helps to prevent leaching of vitamins, especially Vitamin C, and minerals during cooking.

NUTRIENTS
(Average per serve)
Energy 26 kJ (6 kCal)

Nutrient	Amount
Protein	0.66 g
Fat	0.06 g
Carbohydrate	0.72 g
Thiamin	0.01 mg
Riboflavin	0.03 mg
Niacin	0.12 mg
Vitamin C	6.30 mg
Calcium	12.60 mg
Iron	0.30 mg

FRESH PEA PURÉE

from 7–8 months

Peas are usually popular with babies, although they can cause wind.

INGREDIENTS
30 g shelled peas
½ teaspoon water

METHOD
1. Place peas in a small microware bowl with water.
2. Cover and microwave on HIGH (90–100%) for 1 minute.
3. Purée to serve.

VARIATIONS
- For a larger quantity, place 125 g shelled peas in a small container with 2 teaspoons water. Cover and microwave on HIGH (90–100%) for 3 minutes. Purée.
- Add cooked peas to soups, stews and Beginner's Bolognese Sauce (p. 70).
- Mix pea purée with grated cheese.

POINTERS
- Fresh peas take longer to cook than frozen peas as their husks need more cooking before they are soft enough to purée.
- 250 g ready-to-cook frozen peas may be defrosted on HIGH (90–100%) for 3 minutes, in a covered small container. Stir through once.

NUTRIENTS
(Average per serve)
Energy 75 kJ (18 kCal)

Nutrient	Amount
Protein	1.74 g
Fat	0.12 g
Carbohydrate	2.43 g
Thiamin	0.09 mg
Riboflavin	0.04 mg
Niacin	0.69 mg
Vitamin C	9.60 mg
Calcium	9.30 mg
Iron	0.54 mg

CREAMY CAULIFLOWER

from 8 months

This vegetable with its creamy head is low in kilojoules whilst containing good amounts of fibre, Vitamin C and folate. It can cause wind in smaller babies so include in the diet towards the end of the first year. This recipe makes 3 serves.

INGREDIENTS

200 g cauliflower
4–6 tablespoons White Sauce (p. 145) or Cheese Sauce (p. 146)

METHOD

1. Cut cauliflower into florets of the same size.
2. Rinse cauliflower well under running water.
3. Place in a small microwave container with stems facing out.
4. Cover closely with plastic wrap and vent.
5. Microwave on HIGH (90–100%) for 3½ minutes. Stand for 1 minute.
6. Mash or purée with a little white or cheese sauce.

VARIATION

- Broccoli may be cooked in the same way, for children from thirteen months.

POINTERS

- Small florets cook more quickly in the microwave oven than larger pieces.
- Place in a spoke-wheel pattern, with stems facing out, for even cooking.
- Odour left in the oven can be removed by microwaving a bowl of water with lemon slices in it until boiling. Wipe oven clean after.

NUTRIENTS
(Average per serve)
Energy 53 kJ (13 kCal)

Nutrient	Amount
Protein	1.47 g
Fat	0.13 g
Carbohydrate	1.33 g
Thiamin	0.05 mg
Riboflavin	0.07 mg
Niacin	0.27 mg
Vitamin C	37.00 mg
Calcium	8.67 mg
Iron	0.40 mg

FRESH ASPARAGUS

from 10 months

An individual serve of spring asparagus is good for older babies, but a little too fibrous for under ten months.

INGREDIENT

2 thick asparagus stalks, peeled and trimmed

METHOD

1. Wrap the 2 trimmed stalks tightly in plastic wrap.
2. Microwave on HIGH (90–100%) for 15 seconds.
3. Use for finger food when cool.

VARIATIONS

- Use asparagus for dipping into home-made tomato sauce.
- For larger quantities, place 12 medium stalks asparagus, trimmed and rinsed, in a large micro-ware container with tips pointing towards the centre. Drizzle 1 teaspoon melted butter over asparagus and cover container. Microwave on HIGH (90–100%) for 1½–2 minutes. Stand, drain and serve.

POINTERS

- Overcooking vegetables in the microwave oven toughens them. Always weigh asparagus when trimmed to calculate the cooking time so that it is not overcooked.
- If you allow asparagus to stand, it will continue to cook on and soften further.

NUTRIENTS
(Average per serve)
Energy 22 kJ (5 kCal)

Protein	0.78 g
Fat	0.03 g
Carbohydrate	0.44 g
Thiamin	0.05 mg
Riboflavin	0.04 mg
Niacin	0.31 mg
Vitamin C	4.68 mg
Calcium	3.43 mg
Iron	0.31 mg

STEWED APPLE *from 7 months*

Use any variety of apple as it is a high-moisture fruit that cooks quickly and well in the microwave. This recipe makes approximately 2 cups.

INGREDIENTS
4 medium apples (about 500 g)
1 tablespoon water

METHOD
1. Rinse, peel and core apples.
2. Slice thinly and place in the base of a medium-size microware container.
3. Sprinkle with water, cover and place off the centre of the turntable. Microwave on HIGH (90–100%) for 5–6 minutes. Use more or less time depending on the texture desired.
4. Mash with a fork for babies or serve as cooked for older children and the family.

VARIATION
- Pears can be substituted for apples, but more liquid is required. Use 2–3 tablespoons water for 500 g fruit.

FREEZING
- Place in foil tray, 3–4 cm deep with lid. Label and date.
- To defrost, remove lid and place foil container in the centre of the turntable; microwave on DEFROST (30–35%) for 5–7 minutes.

POINTERS
- Sugar is not added to this recipe as the quick microwave cooking highlights the flavour of fruit. If apples are too sour, add a little honey instead of sugar.
- Always cook in a container just large enough to hold the fruit to ensure even results.

NUTRIENTS
(Average per ½ cup)
Energy 230 kJ (55 kCal)

Nutrient	Amount
Protein	0.38 g
Fat	0.00 g
Carbohydrate	13.50 g
Thiamin	0.04 mg
Riboflavin	0.01 mg
Niacin	0.13 mg
Vitamin C	6.25 mg
Calcium	6.25 mg
Iron	0.25 mg

BANANA BUG *from 8–9 months*

Smooth peanut butter spread thinly can be offered to baby from eight months, but definitely not crunchy peanut butter, which can cause choking. Peanut butter in excess is fattening, but it is a good source of protein.

INGREDIENTS

1 ripe banana
1 tablespoon smooth peanut butter

METHOD

1. Peel banana and slice it in half lengthwise.
2. Place it on a plate, cut side down.
3. Lightly spread the peanut butter over the banana.
4. Microwave on HIGH (90–100%) for 1 minute until banana is soft and peanut butter has melted.
5. Stand for 30 seconds before serving.

VARIATION

- Spread smooth peanut butter thinly on toast for baby and offer from eight months.

POINTER

- Baby toast can be made in the microwave oven by placing a slice of white or brown bread on white paper towel and microwaving on HIGH (90–100%) for 2 minutes, turning the bread over once.

NUTRIENTS
(Average per serve)
Energy 1146 kJ (274 kCal)

Nutrient	Amount
Protein	8.03 g
Fat	13.57 g
Carbohydrate	30.98 g
Thiamin	0.11 mg
Riboflavin	0.18 mg
Niacin	4.31 mg
Vitamin C	16.80 mg
Calcium	16.25 mg
Iron	1.22 mg

EGG YOLK CUSTARD

from 9 months

Introduce eggs gradually in the diet, as egg white can cause allergies in some children. However, custards are an ideal alternative way of presenting milk to children, and they include the egg yolk, which is rich in protein and vitamins, while the white is not used. For the best results when cooking custard, all ingredients should be at room temperature.

INGREDIENTS

¼ cup milk (breast or formula)
1 egg yolk

METHOD

1. In a small microware bowl, mix egg yolk well. Add milk, stirring thoroughly.
2. Microwave on LOW (30–40%) for 1 minute. Stir well.
3. Microwave for about a further 1½ minutes on LOW (30–40%), stirring well every 15 seconds, until thick enough to coat spoon.
4. Cool to room temperature to serve.

VARIATION

- Add 1–2 tablespoons of puréed banana to custard.

POINTER

- Hard-cooked eggs can be done in the microwave oven by cracking a room-temperature egg into a custard cup, piercing the yolk, covering with micro-wave-safe plastic wrap and microwaving on MEDIUM (50–60%) for 45–60 seconds. Stand until cool and slice or mash, as desired. The yolk only may be used if preferred.

NUTRIENTS
(Average per serve)
Energy 403 kJ (96 kCal)

Nutrient	Amount
Protein	4.26 g
Fat	6.50 g
Carbohydrate	5.39 g
Thiamin	0.06 mg
Riboflavin	0.13 mg
Niacin	0.52 mg
Vitamin C	3.50 mg
Calcium	71.28 mg
Iron	1.45 mg

YOGHURT JELLY *from 10 months*

A mild flavour and good introduction to both jelly and yoghurt. Makes 2 servings.

INGREDIENTS
½ cup water
1 teaspoon gelatine
60 g tub fruit yoghurt

METHOD
1. Mix ¼ cup water with gelatine in a small microware bowl.
2. Microwave on HIGH (90–100%) for 30 seconds, stirring well.
3. Add remaining water and yoghurt, mix well.
4. Chill to set.

VARIATIONS
- Use yoghurt and cottage cheese blends instead of plain yoghurt.
- Use fruit juice instead of water.
- Add diced fruit to complement the yoghurt.

POINTER
- Gelatine can be dissolved more easily by sprinkling 1 tablespoon over ¼ cup liquid in a microwave-safe bowl and heating on HIGH (90–100%) for 30–40 seconds. Stir until dissolved.

NUTRIENTS
(Average per serve)
Energy 132 kJ (32 kCal)

Nutrient	Amount
Protein	2.55 g
Fat	0.63 g
Carbohydrate	3.72 g
Thiamin	0.03 mg
Riboflavin	0.07 mg
Niacin	0.00 mg
Vitamin C	0.00 mg
Calcium	41.81 mg
Iron	0.11 mg

APPLE JELLY *from 10 months*

Convenient jars of pure apple concentrate are now available in supermarkets. This can be used as a natural sweetener when cooking for baby as it has no additives. Makes 4 serves.

INGREDIENTS
2 cups water
1 tablespoon gelatine
3 teaspoons apple concentrate
green food dye (optional)

METHOD

1. Mix ½ cup water with gelatine in a medium container. Microwave on HIGH (90–100%) for 30 seconds.
2. Add apple concentrate and remaining water. Add 1–2 drops of food dye if desired and stir well.
3. Chill to set.

VARIATION

- Use 1 tablespoon of home-made berry jelly (p. 168) in place of apple concentrate.

POINTERS

- Heat gelatine and liquid in a bowl larger than the volume of fluid as the mixture boils over quickly.
- Apple jelly is a pale colour and many babies eat it more readily if food dye is added.

NUTRIENTS
(Average per serve)
Energy 54 kJ (13 kCal)

Nutrient	Amount
Protein	2.54 g
Fat	0.00 g
Carbohydrate	0.64 g
Thiamin	0.00 mg
Riboflavin	0.00 mg
Niacin	0.02 mg
Vitamin C	2.33 mg
Calcium	6.61 mg
Iron	0.11 mg

CHOC-NANA SMOOTHIE

from 12 months

This delicious drink is high in calcium and phosphorus, two important minerals for bone growth, and also has useful amounts of iron and zinc as well as Vitamin B6. The banana provides complex carbohydrate for energy, and dietary fibre for a healthy gut.

INGREDIENTS

1 banana
1 cup milk
2 tablespoons drinking chocolate powder

METHOD

1. Heat banana in its skin on HIGH (90–100%) for 15 seconds. Knead between the fingers to mash.
2. Heat milk in a small ovenable jug for 1½ minutes on HIGH (90–100%).
3. Blend milk, banana pulp and drinking chocolate until smooth and frothy.

VARIATION

- Use carob powder in place of drinking chocolate.

POINTER

- Bananas can be heated in their skins briefly on HIGH (90–100%) for 15–45 seconds (timing will depend on ripeness) for serving as a warm dessert with custard. Overheating results in blackening and spoiling the fruit.

NUTRIENTS
(Average per serve)
Energy 1822 kJ (435 kCal)

Nutrient	Amount
Protein	13.09 g
Fat	12.34 g
Carbohydrate	70.57 g
Thiamin	0.22 mg
Riboflavin	0.56 mg
Niacin	0.76 mg
Vitamin C	19.38 mg
Calcium	329.80 mg
Iron	1.92 mg

ORANGE JUICE *from 7 months*

Oranges are high in Vitamin C, vital for growing bones, teeth and blood supply. This dilute juice supplements the Vitamin C in breast and formula milk. Home-prepared fresh juice is best, and microwaving the fruit before squeezing allows more juice to be extracted.

INGREDIENT
1 medium orange

METHOD

1. Place orange off the centre of the turntable. Microwave on HIGH (90–100%) for 40 seconds.
2. Allow to stand for 3–4 minutes before squeezing – makes about ¼ cup juice.
3. Dilute 1 teaspoon juice with 8 teaspoons boiled, cooled water (the quantity of orange juice can be gradually increased, as required).

FREEZING

- Whole oranges can be frozen in their skin whilst in season and sweet.
- DEFROST (30-35%) for 40 seconds, then stand several minutes before juicing.

POINTERS

- Whilst oranges are high in Vitamin C they sometimes cause allergies. Introduce gradually to baby.
- Microwave cooking highlights flavours, so do not add sugar to the fresh delights of orange juice.
- Dry the rind of 1 orange by grating peel and spreading evenly on a non-recycled, white paper towel. Cook on HIGH (90–100%) for 2–3 minutes, rearranging several times. Add to cakes or desserts for older children and the rest of the family.

NUTRIENTS
(Average per teaspoon juice, diluted)
Energy 8 kJ (2 kCal)

Protein	0.06 g
Fat	0.01 g
Carbohydrate	0.41 g
Thiamin	0.00 mg
Riboflavin	0.00 mg
Niacin	0.02 mg
Vitamin C	2.65 mg
Calcium	1.25 mg
Iron	0.02 mg

PRUNE JUICE *from 7 months*

Ideal for constipated infants, but 4 teaspoons (diluted with water) is the maximum a baby should have a day, and don't give before seven months. This recipe makes ½ cup.

INGREDIENTS
1 dried prune
½ cup water

METHOD
1. Cut prune in half and place in water in a small container.
2. Microwave on HIGH (90–100%) for 1 minute or until boiling.
3. Strain when cooled. Dilute using 1 teaspoon prune juice to 100 ml of water.

FREEZING
- Fills 5 ice-cube cavities. Freeze until solid. Transfer to microwave-safe plastic bags, label and date and return to freezer.
- DEFROST (30-35%) 1 cube in a microware bowl for 1 minute.

POINTER
- Use your microwave to plump up dried fruit in water quickly - it saves soaking overnight.

Thirteen to eighteen months

The first birthday is a time of real changes. Baby is becoming a toddler, and will be walking and talking soon, if this has not happened already! Weaning will probably be completed, and the molars will start to appear during these months. Baby should get used to chewing food instead of swallowing very soft-textured purées, so gradually move from blending to chopping, and be sure to offer finger-food snacks.

Once young children start running around they tire quickly. It is often easier to get them to eat their main meal in the middle of the day, and a lighter one in the evening when they are feeling tired and less able to concentrate.

Sample meal plan for an eighteen-month-old

Breakfast	Orange Juice (p. 60), Egg Nog (p. 66), 1 slice wholemeal toast with scrape of butter or margarine and Vegemite
Snack	fresh fruit
Lunch	Split Pea Soup (p. 63), Beginner's Bolognese Sauce (p. 70) on pasta with a sprinkle of grated cheese
Snack	Popcorn (p. 169), Lemonade (p. 175)
Dinner	Savoury Custard (p. 80), 1 slice wholemeal bread with scrape of butter or margarine
Snack	Apple Cake (p. 156)

Recommended dietary intake for an average eighteen-month-old

Energy	5720 kJ (1362 kCal)
Protein	15.0 g
Carbohydrate	204 g or less
Fat	at least 53 g
Thiamin	0.6 mg
Riboflavin	0.9 mg
Niacin	9.2 mg
Vitamin C	30.0 mg
Calcium	700.0 mg
Iron	6.0 mg

SPLIT PEA SOUP *from 15 months*

Split peas are the common type of dried peas. They are available in green or yellow varieties and provide an excellent source of protein, iron and fibre, although they are not recommended for babies under twelve months as they are difficult to digest. The recipe makes 150 ml – a single serve.

INGREDIENTS
2 tablespoons green split peas
1 cup hot tap water
1/4 cup chicken stock

METHOD

1. Place peas and water in a small microware container.
2. Microwave on HIGH (90–100%) for 2 minutes. Reduce power to MEDIUM (50–60%) and cook for 15 minutes.
3. Mash peas well. Add stock and serve.

VARIATIONS

- For a creamier soup, blend 1 tablespoon milk powder with a little extra stock and add.
- Use yellow peas and mash with 2 tablespoons carrot purée.

POINTER

- The heat of the cooked peas will be sufficient to warm stock through for infants.

NUTRIENTS
(Average per serve)
Energy 726 kJ (173 kCal)

Nutrient	Amount
Protein	14.53 g
Fat	2.30 g
Carbohydrate	22.45 g
Thiamin	0.14 mg
Riboflavin	0.12 mg
Niacin	2.03 mg
Vitamin C	0.29 mg
Calcium	17.09 mg
Iron	2.13 mg

THE MINUTE MEAL *from 13 months*

If you are on the run, this wholesome meal can be made in the microwave in 60 seconds.

INGREDIENTS

1 × 15 cm diameter cooked crepe
2 tablespoons smooth peanut butter
1 banana

METHOD

1. Spread peanut butter over crepe. Place peeled banana down the centre and roll up firmly.
2. Wrap in baking paper. Place on edge of the turntable. Microwave on MEDIUM (50–60%) for 1 minute, turning once during cooking.
3. Stand for 2 minutes. Serve with yoghurt and drizzle with a little honey or maple syrup, if desired.

VARIATION

- Mountain bread can be used instead of a crepe. Sprinkle rolled bread with a little water and wrap firmly in plastic wrap instead of baking paper. Cook as above.

POINTERS

- Slightly underripe bananas may be softened on LOW (30–40%) for 2–3 minutes each, turning over once during cooking. Cool, and then use as soon as possible. These bananas are not suitable for refrigeration.
- Make a dozen crepes at a time, then freeze in a microwave-safe plastic bag with plastic wrap between them. When you need to use just one, you can remove it easily and DEFROST for 45–60 seconds.

NUTRIENTS
(Average per serve)
Energy 2251 kJ (538 kCal)

Nutrient	Amount
Protein	17.08 g
Fat	31.96 g
Carbohydrate	46.90 g
Thiamin	0.24 mg
Riboflavin	0.37 mg
Niacin	8.66 mg
Vitamin C	16.80 mg
Calcium	85.92 mg
Iron	1.98 mg

WELSH RAREBIT (F)

from 13 months

A traditional meal high in protein and calcium, useful for the growing bones of babies and toddlers. Makes 4 rarebits.

INGREDIENTS

¼ cup milk
1 cup grated cheddar cheese
1 egg, lightly beaten
mustard (optional)

METHOD

1. Bring milk to the boil in a small microware container on HIGH (90–100%) for 1 minute.
2. Add cheese and stir well to melt.
3. Add egg and a touch of mustard if desired. Stir well.
4. Microwave on MEDIUM (50–60%) for 1½ minutes, stirring every 15 seconds.
5. Pour over toast or muffins; sprinkle with a little parsley to serve.

VARIATION

- Keep chilled and use as a sandwich filling for older children.

POINTERS

- Grated cheese melts more evenly than chunks in the microwave.
- Overcooked cheese becomes tough and stringy. To avoid this, use MEDIUM (50–60%) or LOW (30–40%) power.

NUTRIENTS
(Average per serve)
Energy 747 kJ (178 kCal)

Nutrient	Amount
Protein	11.58 g
Fat	14.50 g
Carbohydrate	0.82 g
Thiamin	0.02 mg
Riboflavin	0.26 mg
Niacin	0.08 mg
Vitamin C	0.16 mg
Calcium	313.90 mg
Iron	0.32 mg

EGG NOG *from 13 months*

An easy whole meal for the winter blues, and a good way of slipping an egg into baby's diet if junior is not keen.

INGREDIENTS

1 cup milk
1 egg, lightly beaten
nutmeg
½ teaspoon honey (optional)

METHOD

1. Heat milk in a medium microware container or jug on HIGH (90–100%) for 2 minutes.
2. Whisk in egg and a pinch of nutmeg. Sweeten with honey, if necessary.

VARIATION

■ Use vanilla essence in place of nutmeg.

POINTER

■ Milk boils over, so always heat in a container which is twice the size of the quantity to be cooked.

NUTRIENTS
(Average per serve)
Energy 1026 kJ (245 kCal)

Nutrient	Amount
Protein	14.62 g
Fat	14.65 g
Carbohydrate	14.59 g
Thiamin	0.16 mg
Riboflavin	0.59 mg
Niacin	0.01 mg
Vitamin C	2.58 mg
Calcium	328.49 mg
Iron	1.04 mg

BAKED RICOTTA MOUNDS

from 13 months

Fresh ricotta is cheese in its simplest form, or at its closest to milk. It mixes well with many foods. This dish is rich in calcium, from the tuna and ricotta, protein and B vitamins.

INGREDIENTS

3 tablespoons smooth ricotta cheese
1 egg, lightly beaten
2 tablespoons flaked, cooked or canned tuna

METHOD

1. Beat cheese and egg well in a small microware bowl. Add tuna and mix well.
2. Microwave on MEDIUM (50–60%) for 3 minutes or until set.
3. Stand for 5 minutes.
4. Turn out to serve with toast or salad.

POINTER

■ Overcooked cheese becomes tough and stringy so always use MEDIUM (50–60%) or LOW (30–40%) power when cooking it.

NUTRIENTS
(Average per serve)
Energy 812 kJ (194 kCal)

Nutrient	Amount
Protein	19.94 g
Fat	12.42 g
Carbohydrate	0.86 g
Thiamin	0.05 mg
Riboflavin	0.36 mg
Niacin	2.43 mg
Vitamin C	0.00 mg
Calcium	156.17 mg
Iron	1.28 mg

TUNA CASSEROLE (F)

from 13 months

Tuna is nutritious – providing vitamins B, D and E – and economical family fare. Keep a can in the cupboard so you can make a meal quickly. This recipe is sufficient for 4 people; baby's portion is removed before seasoning.

INGREDIENTS

1 small onion, finely chopped
30 g butter
3 tablespoons flour
1 cup milk
1 × 180 g can tuna, in salt-reduced brine
1 × 130 g can creamed corn
1 cup cooked rice
1–2 teaspoons chopped fresh parsley
1 tablespoon lemon juice
1/3 cup cornflakes

METHOD

1. Place onion and butter in a medium-size microware container and cook on HIGH (90–100%) for 1½ minutes.
2. Stir in flour and cook for 30 seconds on HIGH (90–100%).
3. Drain tuna, reserving liquid, and make liquid up to ½ cup with water. Add to flour and onion and stir well. Stir in milk.
4. Cook for 2 minutes on HIGH (90–100%), stirring well. Cook another 2 minutes on HIGH (90–100%), stirring well every 30 seconds.
5. Add corn, tuna, rice and parsley. Mix thoroughly. Microwave on HIGH (90–100%) for 1 minute, stirring occasionally.
6. Remove child's portion. Add lemon juice and season to taste with freshly ground pepper. Microwave on HIGH (90–100%) for 1 minute.
7. Lightly crush cornflakes in your hand and sprinkle on top to serve.

FREEZING

- Freeze in ½ cup portions.
- DEFROST (30-35%) in microware bowl for 3½ minutes per portion.

POINTER

- When reheating a cup of refrigerated rice, always add a tablespoon of water or stock to keep it moist.

NUTRIENTS
(Average per serve)
Energy 1211 kJ (289 kCal)

Nutrient	Amount
Protein	15.39 g
Fat	10.44 g
Carbohydrate	33.34 g
Thiamin	0.15 mg
Riboflavin	0.22 mg
Niacin	4.73 mg
Vitamin C	5.80 mg
Calcium	90.23 mg
Iron	1.25 mg

BONZA BEEF STEW (F)

from 13 months

Lean beef is low in fat and contains only moderate amounts of cholesterol while being a good source of protein, iron and zinc, so include beef in your weekly meal plan for baby. This recipe is also rich in Vitamin A, and the pasta provides carbohydrate for energy. Serves 4.

INGREDIENTS

500 g blade or round steak, cut into 3-cm cubes
3 tomatoes, skinned and chopped
1 small onion, finely diced or grated
2 sticks celery, thinly sliced
1 tablespoon finely chopped parsley
2 cups hot beef stock
1 cup cooked pasta shells

METHOD

1. In a 4-cup ovenable jug heat beef stock on HIGH (90–100%) for 5 minutes.
2. Place cut vegetables in the lid of a large microware container, cover with plastic wrap and blanch on HIGH (90–100%) for 5 minutes.
3. Pierce and pound beef. Place cubes into the large microware container. Add vegetables and parsley. Pour over hot beef stock. Cover.
4. Place in the centre of the turntable and microwave on HIGH (90–100%) for 5 minutes, then reduce power to MEDIUM (50–60%) for 15 minutes.
5. Stir, re-cover and reduce power to DEFROST (30–35%) for 5–10 minutes, until skewer-soft.
6. Stand for 5 minutes. Stir in pasta shells. Remove a serve for baby and blend to a chunky consistency with stock.

VARIATION

- Cooked potato cubes may be added in place of pasta.

POINTERS

- To skin a tomato easily heat on HIGH (90–100%) for 45 seconds (until skin splits). Stand for 2–3 minutes, then peel.
- Hot stock speeds up the cooking time.

NUTRIENTS
(Average per serve)
Energy 1004 kJ (240 kCal)

Protein	31.88 g
Fat	6.56 g
Carbohydrate	12.89 g
Thiamin	0.17 mg
Riboflavin	0.29 mg
Niacin	6.83 mg
Vitamin C	22.55 mg
Calcium	45.54 mg
Iron	3.49 mg

BEGINNER'S BOLOGNESE SAUCE (F)

from 15 months

Spaghetti is fun to eat, especially if topped with bolognese sauce made from lean veal, which has a light flavour and smooth texture. Younger children sometimes find long spaghetti strands hard to manage, and prefer smaller twists or shell pasta. This recipe makes enough sauce for the whole family.

INGREDIENTS

1 onion, finely chopped
500 g minced veal
750 g tomatoes, skinned and chopped
4–5 bay leaves
1/8 teaspoon each dried ground oregano and basil
1 × 140 g tub tomato paste
1 clove garlic (optional)

METHOD

1. Place onion in a large microware container. Cover, microwave on HIGH (90–100%) for 1 minute.
2. Stir meat into onion. Cook on HIGH (90–100%) for 1 minute, stirring occasionally.
3. Add chopped tomatoes and herbs. Stir well. Cover. Cook on MEDIUM (50–60%) for 20 minutes, stirring several times.
4. Remove bay leaves, stir in tomato paste thoroughly. Remove infant's serve. Add crushed garlic and additional herbs to flavour. Serve on pasta of choice (see Faster Pasta, p. 96, for cooking method).

VARIATIONS

- Add 100 g sliced mushrooms with chopped tomatoes.
- Beef can be used but veal is lean and tender for young children.

FREEZING

- Freeze in ½ cup portions.
- DEFROST (30-35%) for 4 minutes per ½ cup.

POINTERS

- Cook bolognese sauce in an ovenable glass jug for easy cleaning.
- To skin a tomato easily, slash and heat tomato on HIGH (90–100%) for 45 seconds. Stand for 2–3 minutes, then peel.

NUTRIENTS
(Average per ½ cup)
Energy 390 kJ (93 kCal)

Nutrient	Amount
Protein	16.18 g
Fat	1.05 g
Carbohydrate	4.44 g
Thiamin	0.19 mg
Riboflavin	0.23 mg
Niacin	4.21 mg
Vitamin C	35.43 mg
Calcium	22.90 mg
Iron	2.23 mg

RACK OF LAMB (F)

from 15 months

Enjoy a roast dinner in just ten minutes! Lamb is a soft meat that can easily be cut into small mouthfuls, while some children love chewing the bone. Cut a chop off the end of a cooked rack for baby.

INGREDIENTS

2 × 4-cutlet racks of lamb
2 teaspoons honey
2 teaspoons light soy sauce
1 teaspoon cornflour
1 tablespoon water

METHOD

1. Trim lamb well of fat and sinew. Mix honey and soy together. Brush glaze on lamb. (Adult lamb can be studded with garlic.)
2. Place lamb on roasting rack or ovenable glass pie dish. Cover with piece of paper towel and microwave on MEDIUM (50–60%) for 7 minutes. Stand for 2 minutes.
3. Remove lamb to serving plate. Blend cornflour with water to dissolve. Add to meat juice. Stir well.
4. Microwave on HIGH (90–100%) for approximately 1 minute, stirring regularly, until thickened. Pour over meat.

VARIATION

- Adults may like to mix equal proportions of soy sauce and their favourite mustard as a glaze for lamb.

FREEZING

- Place leftover meat with two vegetables and a little gravy on a plain dinner plate. Wrap in microwave-safe plastic and freeze, ready to defrost on a busy day.
- DEFROST (30-35%) for 2-3 minutes.

POINTERS

- For a mini roast: cook small quantities of meat on MEDIUM (50–60%) to prevent toughening.
- Thin honey in the microwave on HIGH (90–100%) for 30 seconds for easier mixing.
- Plain paper towel absorbs splatters and keeps the microwave clean.

NUTRIENTS
(Average per cutlet)
Energy 814 kJ (194 kCal)

Nutrient	Amount
Protein	22.79 g
Fat	10.81 g
Carbohydrate	1.72 g
Thiamin	0.05 mg
Riboflavin	0.18 mg
Niacin	3.86 mg
Vitamin C	0.00 mg
Calcium	9.85 mg
Iron	2.15 mg

SAUCY RABBIT (F)

from 13 months

Australians are ambivalent about eating rabbit, which is a shame as it is low in cholesterol, mild in flavour, always available and inexpensive. It provides protein, B vitamins, iron and phosphorus. A creamy sauce makes this a budget meal for 4.

INGREDIENTS

1 medium rabbit (about 850 g), cleaned and cut into 8 portions
1 carrot, chopped roughly
1 white onion, quartered
1 bay leaf
2 cups hot water
100 g frozen peas
2 cups White Sauce (p. 145)
2 tablespoons finely chopped parsley

METHOD

1. Soak rabbit for at least 6 hours in the refrigerator in slightly salted water. Drain, dry and pierce pieces.
2. Put into a large container with carrot, onion and bay leaf. Pour over hot water, cover and place in the centre of the turntable.
3. Microwave on HIGH (90–100%) for 10 minutes, then reduce power to DEFROST (30–35%) and cook another 15 minutes.
4. Stir, ensuring rabbit pieces are turned over. Recover and microwave on DEFROST (30–35%) for 15 minutes. Stand for 5 minutes. Rabbit should be skewer-soft. Pour off liquid, reserving some.
5. When cool, discard bones. Cut meat into small pieces. Remove child's serve; blend to a chunky consistency with the reserved stock.
6. Place rabbit pieces with carrot and frozen peas in container. Pour over white sauce. Reheat, covered, on MEDIUM (50–60%) for 7–10 minutes. Garnish with parsley. Serve with rice.

POINTER

■ When stirring, make sure you move the outer pieces of rabbit to the centre and vice versa, for even cooking results.

NUTRIENTS
(Average per serve)
Energy 1556 kJ (372 kCal)

Protein	34.08 g
Fat	20.99 g
Carbohydrate	12.16 g
Thiamin	0.22 mg
Riboflavin	0.52 mg
Niacin	9.23 mg
Vitamin C	8.33 mg
Calcium	189.70 mg
Iron	2.79 mg

CHICKEN AND APPLE PÂTÉ

from 15 months

Liver is not always popular in families but a little creative cooking makes a difference. Try mixing liver with fruit, it tastes surprisingly good! This recipe makes 2 cups.

INGREDIENTS
1 small onion, chopped
2 tablespoons chicken stock
200 g chicken livers, chopped
1 red apple, peeled and grated
2 teaspoons tomato paste
2 tablespoons cream or yoghurt

METHOD

1. Place onion and stock in a small microware container. Cover, microwave on HIGH (90–100%) for 1 minute.
2. Add chopped livers and peeled and grated apple. Cover, cook on MEDIUM (50–60%) for 5 minutes, stirring regularly.
3. Purée liver mixture with tomato paste and cream. Chill, covered, to store.

VARIATION

- If you have not got any pre-made stock available, apple juice may be used. It can be seasoned with ground cloves.

POINTER

- Avoid tears when peeling onions. Trim the ends off. Place onion on paper towel on the turntable. Heat on HIGH (90–100%) for 1 minute. Remove the skin, slice or chop without watering eyes.

NUTRIENTS
(Average per 25 g)
Energy 139 kJ (33 kCal)

Nutrient	Amount
Protein	3.18 g
Fat	1.96 g
Carbohydrate	0.76 g
Thiamin	0.03 mg
Riboflavin	0.38 mg
Niacin	1.36 mg
Vitamin C	3.29 mg
Calcium	3.88 mg
Iron	1.37 mg

KIDNEY AND VEGETABLE FRICASSEE

from 13 months

This mixture should be nice and tender, so it can be mashed. High in protein, vitamins and minerals, kidneys are inexpensive and healthy. Carrots provide Vitamin A, and peas contribute iron. The white sauce adds calcium, making this a delicious, well-rounded meal. Makes 2–3 portions.

INGREDIENTS

1 lamb's kidney, halved, soaked, cleaned and diced
3 tablespoons water
½ carrot, diced
½ cup frozen peas
2 tablespoons thick White Sauce (p. 145)

METHOD

1. Place kidney and 2 tablespoons water in microware bowl, cover and microwave on MEDIUM (50–60%) for 3 minutes, stirring once. Drain kidney and set aside.
2. Place carrot in microware bowl with 1 tablespoon water and microwave on HIGH (90–100%) for 2 minutes. Add frozen peas and microwave on HIGH (90–100%) for a further minute. Drain.
3. Mix kidneys and vegetables together, pour over white sauce and reheat on MEDIUM-HIGH (70–80%) for 2 minutes, stirring once.
4. Refrigerate, covered, for other meals.

VARIATION

- For older children add 1 tablespoon of grated cheese.

POINTER

- To cook 500 g kidneys: halve, pierce and microwave on HIGH (90–100%) for 5–6 minutes.

NUTRIENTS
(Average per serve)
Energy 566 kJ (135 kCal)

Nutrient	Amount
Protein	9.21 g
Fat	7.39 g
Carbohydrate	8.27 g
Thiamin	0.28 mg
Riboflavin	0.67 mg
Niacin	2.71 mg
Vitamin C	10.44 mg
Calcium	102.10 mg
Iron	3.29 mg

RICE

from 13 months

Rice is the main food crop for half the world's population and it cooks well in the microwave. It is rich in carbohydrate and B vitamins, making it an excellent energy source, and brown rice contains plenty of fibre for healthy bowels. You can refrigerate or freeze cooked rice and then reheat it in mere minutes as required. Two tablespoons of uncooked rice make ½ cup.

INGREDIENTS

White Rice

¾ cup lukewarm water
2 tablespoons long-grain white rice, washed

Brown Rice

2 cups lukewarm water
2 tablespoons long-grain brown rice, washed

METHOD

1. Bring water to the boil in a small microware container on HIGH (90–100%) – ¾ cup water will take 1½ minutes, 2 cups 3 minutes.
2. Add rice. Cook white rice for 9–10 minutes or brown rice for 20 minutes on HIGH (90–100%), until rice is cooked and water absorbed.

VARIATIONS

- Make Fried Rice (p. 106).
- Add rice to Baked Egg Custard (p. 81) or fish casseroles.

FREEZING

- Place cooked rice in microwave-safe freezer bags in serving portions, convenient for your family.
- DEFROST (30-35%) 1 cup cooked frozen rice for 5 minutes. Adjust timing for smaller or larger amounts.

POINTER

- To cook a larger quantity: take 1 cup white rice, add 1¾ cups lukewarm water and a teaspoon light oil. Microwave in medium microware container, uncovered, off the centre of the turntable for 10 minutes on HIGH (90–100%) or until the water has absorbed. Fork through, cover, and let stand for 3 minutes. Serves 3-4.

NUTRIENTS
(Average per ½ cup)
Energy 484 kJ (116 kCal)

Nutrient	Amount
Protein	2.16 g
Fat	0.16 g
Carbohydrate	25.94 g
Thiamin	0.03 mg
Riboflavin	0.01 mg
Niacin	0.66 mg
Vitamin C	0.00 mg
Calcium	2.30 mg
Iron	0.23 mg

BROCCOLI *from 13 months*

Cooked in the microwave, broccoli becomes a wonderful emerald green. It is one of the most nutritious vegetables, being a good source of vitamins A and C and containing calcium and iron.

INGREDIENTS
200 g broccoli
2–3 tablespoons White Sauce (p. 145)

METHOD
1. Cut broccoli into florets of equal size. Rinse.
2. Place in a small microware container with stems facing out. Cover closely with plastic wrap and vent.
3. Microwave on HIGH (90–100%) for 3 minutes. Stand for 1 minute.
4. Mash well with a little white sauce to serve.

VARIATION
- Top with grated mozzarella cheese.

POINTERS
- Broccoli is cooked after 2 minutes, but not sufficiently to mash.
- Odour in the oven can be removed by washing out the interior with vinegar or vanilla-flavoured water.

NUTRIENTS
(Average per serve)
Energy 202 kJ (48 kCal)

Nutrient	Amount
Protein	9.40 g
Fat	0.60 g
Carbohydrate	0.80 g
Thiamin	0.14 mg
Riboflavin	0.42 mg
Niacin	1.00 mg
Vitamin C	170.00 mg
Calcium	58.00 mg
Iron	2.00 mg

CAULIFLOWER, CARROT AND CORN COMBO (F)

from 13 months

Cauliflower is a member of the cabbage family and when cooked conventionally releases unpleasant sulphur compounds during cooking. By using your microwave oven, kitchen odours are kept to a minimum. Makes 4 serves for a family meal.

POINTER

■ Cut through stems of cauliflower and place stems outwards in a dish to ensure even cooking.

INGREDIENTS

200 g cauliflower
125 g carrot
1 teaspoon water
1 × 130 g can creamed corn
2 eggs, beaten
parmesan cheese

METHOD

1. Cut cauliflower into florets of equal size. Rinse. Place in a small microware container, cover and vent. Microwave on HIGH (90–100%) for 3½ minutes.
2. Peel and slice carrot. Place in a small microware container with 1 teaspoon of water. Cover. Microwave on HIGH (90–100%) for 3 minutes.
3. Mash carrot, cauliflower, corn and eggs together.
4. Pour into a small microware container. Microwave on MEDIUM (50–60%) for 10 minutes, or until set.
5. Stand for 5 minutes. Sprinkle parmesan on servings for adults.

VARIATION

■ Use broccoli in place of cauliflower.

NUTRIENTS
(Average per serve)
Energy 397 kJ (95 kCal)

Protein	5.34 g
Fat	3.17 g
Carbohydrate	11.21 g
Thiamin	0.11 mg
Riboflavin	0.18 mg
Niacin	1.04 mg
Vitamin C	30.55 mg
Calcium	25.90 mg
Iron	0.94 mg

BUBBLE AND SQUEAK SLICE

from 13 months

A great way to use up leftover vegetables from family meals. It is also terrific nutritionally for toddlers, the vegetables providing vitamins A and C, iron, zinc and fibre, while the egg and cheese add protein and valuable calcium. This recipe makes 6–8 slices.

INGREDIENTS

1 cup cooked potato, mashed or puréed
1 cup cooked pumpkin, mashed or puréed
1 cup cooked spinach or peas, mashed
1 egg
½ cup grated cheese

METHOD

1. Combine potato, pumpkin and greens, mashing thoroughly.
2. Stir in egg and blend well.
3. Spread mix in the base of a large microware container and cover.
4. Place in the centre of the turntable and microwave on HIGH (90–100%) for 5 minutes.
5. Sprinkle cheese over top of slice, re-cover container and microwave on MEDIUM (50–60%) for 1 minute.
6. Stand for 2 minutes, then cut into wedges.

VARIATION

- Substitute parsnip or carrot purée for potato or pumpkin.

POINTER

- Frozen spinach or peas can be used in this recipe. Defrost 250 g peas on HIGH (90–100%) for 3 minutes, or 250 g spinach on HIGH (90–100%) for 5 minutes.

NUTRIENTS
(Average per slice)
Energy 496 kJ (119 kCal)

Nutrient	Amount
Protein	7.89 g
Fat	8.07 g
Carbohydrate	3.77 g
Thiamin	0.07 mg
Riboflavin	0.18 mg
Niacin	0.46 mg
Vitamin C	6.71 mg
Calcium	174.97 mg
Iron	0.72 mg

VEGETABLE SCRAMBLE

from 13 months

Clean up the tail end of refrigerated vegies with this healthy egg scramble.

INGREDIENTS

1 tablespoon grated carrot
1 tablespoon grated zucchini
1 tablespoon creamed corn
1 egg, lightly beaten
1 tablespoon milk or water
1 tablespoon grated cheddar cheese

METHOD

1. Place carrot and zucchini in a small bowl. Cover with plastic wrap. Microwave on HIGH (90–100%) for 1 minute.
2. Add corn, egg and milk or water. Stir thoroughly and microwave, uncovered, on HIGH (90–100%) for 30–40 seconds, stirring twice during cooking.
3. Sprinkle with cheese. Stand for 1 minute. Serve with toast.

POINTER

■ Blanching vegetables briefly before adding to eggs, casseroles or sauces ensures they cook sufficiently in the short cooking times of the microwave.

NUTRIENTS
(Average per serve)
Energy 855 kJ (204 kCal)

Nutrient	Amount
Protein	13.88 g
Fat	14.37 g
Carbohydrate	5.20 g
Thiamin	0.07 mg
Riboflavin	0.37 mg
Niacin	0.45 mg
Vitamin C	3.77 mg
Calcium	242.23 mg
Iron	1.01 mg

SAVOURY CUSTARD

from 13 months

A nutritious way of enlarging baby's menu. As well as fibre and vitamins A and C provided by the vegetables, the milk and cheese ensure a good amount of protein, and calcium and phosphorus to keep bones and teeth healthy.

INGREDIENTS

1 egg, lightly beaten
½ cup milk
2 tablespoons cooked, mashed vegetable (pumpkin, carrots or sprouts, or a mixture of two)
1 tablespoon grated cheddar cheese

METHOD

1. Mix egg, milk and vegetables together well.
2. Pour into a small microware bowl and stir in cheese.
3. Microwave on LOW (30–40%) for 3 minutes.
4. Stand for 1 minute, then cook a further 2½–3 minutes on LOW (30–40%).
5. Stand for 5 minutes. Serve warm.

VARIATION

- Use mozzarella cheese instead of cheddar.

POINTER

- Finely grated moist cheese is easier to mix through baby's recipes and cooks more evenly than larger, harder pieces.

NUTRIENTS
(Average per serve)
Energy 1103 kJ (264 kCal)

Nutrient	Amount
Protein	17.98 g
Fat	18.28 g
Carbohydrate	7.43 g
Thiamin	0.14 mg
Riboflavin	0.57 mg
Niacin	0.51 mg
Vitamin C	12.87 mg
Calcium	377.49 mg
Iron	1.39 mg

BAKED EGG CUSTARD

from 13 months

Eggs are adaptable. Sweet or savoury meals can be made up in minutes. They are also a wonderful source of proteins, minerals, vitamins and iron. Makes 1 portion.

INGREDIENTS

1 egg, lightly beaten
1/2 cup milk
1/8 teaspoon sugar (optional)
1 drop vanilla essence

METHOD

1. Mix egg, milk, sugar (omit sugar for an unsweetened custard) and vanilla essence in a small microware bowl and microwave on LOW (30–40%) for 3 minutes.
2. Stand for 1 minute, then cook a further 2–2½ minutes on LOW (30–40%).
3. Stand for 5 minutes.
4. Serve warm or cold.

VARIATIONS

- Add 2 tablespoons stewed fruit (pears or apricots) to the mixture before cooking.
- Add 1 tablespoon cooked rice and 1 tablespoon sultanas to the mixture.
- Top cooked custard with All Seasons Fruit Sauce (p. 153).

POINTER

- **Custards cook best in the microwave if all the ingredients are at room temperature.**

NUTRIENTS
(Average per serve)
Energy 642 kJ (153 kCal)

Protein	10.35 g
Fat	9.75 g
Carbohydrate	6.53 g
Thiamin	0.10 mg
Riboflavin	0.39 mg
Niacin	0.00 mg
Vitamin C	1.29 mg
Calcium	173.53 mg
Iron	0.90 mg

APPLE ISLES *from 13 months*

Save yourself three-quarters of an hour cooking time with this dessert, and the kids will have fun watching it cook. Makes 2 serves.

INGREDIENTS
1 egg white
1 teaspoon sugar
2 tablespoons apple purée

METHOD
1. Whip egg white until stiff. Add sugar and mix well. Add apple purée and beat well to mix.
2. Using a microwave-safe flat dish, or container cover, spoon mixture into two oval mounds and level the tops with a spatula.
3. Microwave on MEDIUM (50–60%) for 45 seconds, until peaks form and set. Serve hot or cold with yoghurt.

VARIATION
- Use apricot, pear, rhubarb or banana purée in place of apple.

FREEZING
- Freeze egg white in ice-cube cavities.
- Thaw 1 frozen egg white on DEFROST (30-35%) for 1 minute.

POINTER
- Refrigerated apple isles will need to be drained before serving.

NUTRIENTS
(Average per serve)
Energy 121 kJ (29 kCal)

Nutrient	Amount
Protein	1.80 g
Fat	0.00 g
Carbohydrate	5.53 g
Thiamin	0.01 mg
Riboflavin	0.07 mg
Niacin	0.02 mg
Vitamin C	2.37 mg
Calcium	1.46 mg
Iron	0.07 mg

RHUBARB AND APPLE CRUMBLE

from 13 months

Well-trimmed rhubarb stalks make a tangy dessert pie. Serves 2–3.

INGREDIENTS

3 rhubarb stalks
2 apples
1 teaspoon sugar
¼ cup wholemeal self-raising flour
20 g butter
1 tablespoon dark brown sugar

METHOD

1. Remove any leaves and base of stalk from rhubarb. Cut into 2-cm pieces.
2. Peel, core and slice apples.
3. Place fruit and teaspoon sugar in a medium microware container. Cover with lid. Cook on HIGH (90–100%) for 5 minutes, stirring occasionally.
4. Rub butter into flour to resemble fine breadcrumbs. Add brown sugar, mix well.
5. Sprinkle crumble mixture over fruit. Cook on HIGH (90–100%) for 2 minutes.
6. Stand for 5 minutes before serving with yoghurt, custard or ice cream in small bowls.

VARIATIONS

- Double the quantity for family fare and increase the cooking time.
- Apple crumble can be made using 500 g apples only.

POINTER

- Cook 500 g trimmed rhubarb stalks, cut into 3-cm pieces, in 2 tablespoons of the juice of your choice on HIGH (90–100%), uncovered, for 6–7 minutes. Sweeten to taste.

NUTRIENTS
(Average per serve)
Energy 492 kJ (118 kCal)

Nutrient	Amount
Protein	1.91 g
Fat	4.39 g
Carbohydrate	17.22 g
Thiamin	0.10 mg
Riboflavin	0.03 mg
Niacin	0.86 mg
Vitamin C	6.13 mg
Calcium	16.62 mg
Iron	0.53 mg

CREAMED RICE *from 13 months*

The versatility of rice cannot be underestimated. Cooked with milk, it forms the base of a variety of sweet treats.

INGREDIENTS
1 cup milk
1 tablespoon white, roundgrain rice
apple concentrate or honey (optional)
cinnamon sugar

METHOD
1. Place milk and rice in a medium microware container. Microwave on HIGH (90–100%) for 2½ minutes or until boiling. Stir.
2. Reduce power to MEDIUM (50–60%), microwave for 12 minutes, stirring every 2 minutes. Sweeten with a little apple concentrate or honey, if necessary.
3. Stand for 5 minutes. Sprinkle with a little cinnamon sugar.

VARIATIONS
- After standing stir in a tablespoon of fruit yoghurt.
- Add a few sultanas or chopped dried apricot before standing.
- Add some sliced or mashed banana.

POINTER
- Large containers prevent milk boiling over.

NUTRIENTS
(Average per serve)
Energy 941 kJ (225 kCal)

Protein	9.60 g
Fat	9.89 g
Carbohydrate	24.84 g
Thiamin	0.14 mg
Riboflavin	0.39 mg
Niacin	0.33 mg
Vitamin C	2.58 mg
Calcium	310.75 mg
Iron	0.37 mg

ORANGE JELLY *from 13 months*

Babies enjoy fruit jellies and they are simple to make with fresh fruit juice. This makes 1½ cups of jelly – about 2–3 serves.

INGREDIENTS

1 orange
1 tablespoon gelatine
1¼ cups water
1 teaspoon sugar
red and yellow food dye (optional)

METHOD

1. Squeeze juice from orange. Put in a small container and make up to ¾ cup with water.
2. Add gelatine to juice, stir well. Microwave on HIGH (90–100%) for 30 seconds.
3. Add sugar and remaining water. Add a drop each of red and yellow food dye for a more orange-coloured jelly.
4. Chill until set.

VARIATIONS

- Use half orange and half lemon juice, with a little more sugar.
- For a stronger flavour, use 1 cup orange juice and 1 cup water.

POINTER

- To extract the maximum juice from an orange, heat fruit in the microwave oven for 30–40 seconds on HIGH (90–100%). Stand, then squeeze.

NUTRIENTS
(Average per serve)
Energy 233 kJ (56 kCal)

Nutrient	Amount
Protein	5.82 g
Fat	0.08 g
Carbohydrate	7.68 g
Thiamin	0.08 mg
Riboflavin	0.02 mg
Niacin	0.15 mg
Vitamin C	39.00 mg
Calcium	35.41 mg
Iron	0.48 mg

HOME-MADE YOGHURT (F)

from 13 months

Yoghurt has the reputation of being a healthy food and it is easy to digest. It is an excellent basic food for the family and an easy early food for baby as it mixes well with fruit or carob, or can be frozen into ice-blocks for toddlers.

INGREDIENTS

2 cups milk
2 tablespoons milk powder
1 tablespoon plain yoghurt

METHOD

1. Mix milk and milk powder together thoroughly.
2. Microwave on HIGH (90–100%) for 4½ minutes, to just under boiling point.
3. Allow to cool to body temperature, approximately 38°. Keep covered while cooking to prevent skin forming.
4. Sterilise a thermos.
5. Mix yoghurt into milk thoroughly. Pour yoghurt mixture into thermos, close lid and leave for approximately 8 hours or overnight, until set. Refrigerate when set.

VARIATION

- Add some stewed fruit or jam to make fruit yoghurt. Some fruits may need the addition of gelatine to help set.

POINTERS

- Reserve 2 tablespoons home-made yoghurt to continue making your own.
- Home-made yoghurt should be eaten within a few days.
- The freshest milk, powder and yoghurt will result in your yoghurt setting quicker.
- If yoghurt does not set after making your own on the fourth or fifth time, try using bought yoghurt to start the process again.

NUTRIENTS
(Average per 100 g)
Energy 325 kJ (78 kCal)

Nutrient	Amount
Protein	4.09 g
Fat	4.47 g
Carbohydrate	5.56 g
Thiamin	0.06 mg
Riboflavin	0.20 mg
Niacin	0.05 mg
Vitamin C	1.01 mg
Calcium	142.23 mg
Iron	0.10 mg

HOT HONEY-LEMON DRINK

from 13 months

Over the centuries honey has been used as a sweetener and many claims have been made for its therapeutic qualities. This old-fashioned cure for colds is good for wet winter days too.

INGREDIENTS
1 small lemon
2/3 cup water
1 tablespoon honey

METHOD
1. Heat lemon on HIGH (90–100%) for 30–40 seconds, stand, then squeeze.
2. Heat water in a microware cup or glass for 1 minute on HIGH (90–100%).
3. Add lemon juice and honey, stir well.

FREEZING
- You can freeze individual lemons in their skins.
- DEFROST (30-35%) lemon for 1 minute. Stand for 1 minute.

NUTRIENTS
(Average per serve)
Energy 347 kJ (83 kCal)

Nutrient	Amount
Protein	0.26 g
Fat	0.00 g
Carbohydrate	21.43 g
Thiamin	0.01 mg
Riboflavin	0.02 mg
Niacin	0.10 mg
Vitamin C	25.00 mg
Calcium	5.35 mg
Iron	0.16 mg

BARLEY WATER *from 13 months*

Barley has long held a reputation as a healthful grain, but it is only in recent years that its true contribution to nutrition has been recognised. Barley contains fibre, B vitamins and minerals, but my grandmother always thought upon it as the ideal base for a cool drink, especially if you were feeling a 'bit off colour'.

INGREDIENTS

2 tablespoons pearl barley
4 cups hot water
rind of 2 lemons, without pith
juice of 2 lemons

METHOD

1. Place barley, water and lemon rind in a 4-cup ovenable glass jug. Cover with vented plastic wrap.
2. Place in the centre of the turntable and microwave on HIGH (90–100%) for 10 minutes.
3. Reduce power to DEFROST (30–35%) and microwave for 45 minutes.
4. Drain barley water through a fine sieve, add the lemon juice, cool and then refrigerate in a covered container until ready to use.

VARIATION

- Barley water may be sweetened with honey, if desired.

POINTER

- Maximise the juice from lemons by placing individual lemons into the microwave and heating on HIGH (90–100%) for 30–40 seconds. Stand for 2–3 minutes and then juice.

Nineteen to twenty-four months

Toddlers are unpredictable. One week they may only want to eat bread and fruit, then the next week they will only touch cereal and meat. Some weeks they may not seem to eat much at all. Don't worry. Children will get enough nourishment in their own particular way. It is important, though, to ensure they have regular mealtimes and don't just snack when *they* want. Now is the time, too, to introduce different tastes. Children are conservative creatures, and you may find a two-year-old refusing to try anything new – so make sure your toddler is used to a wide variety of flavours and textures now.

Sample diet plan for an average two-year-old

Breakfast	2 Weetbix or 1 cup wholegrain cereal with milk, Orange Juice (p. 60)
Snack	Peanut Butter Cookie (p. 163), 1 glass milk
Lunch	Tuna Boats (p. 116), Three Milks Ice Cream (p. 140) with fresh blueberries
Snack	Banana Muffin (p. 165)
Dinner	Pork Hot Pot (p. 126), Rice (p. 75), Peach Sponge Pudding (p. 142)
Snack	fresh fruit

Always offer glasses of cool water through the day as well as milk or juices and put a water jug on the table at mealtimes.

Recommended dietary intake for an average two-year-old

Energy	6240 kJ (1486 kCal)
Protein	16.0 g
Carbohydrate	225 g or less
Fat	at least 58 g
Thiamin	0.6 mg
Riboflavin	0.9 mg
Niacin	10.0 mg
Vitamin C	30.0 mg
Calcium	700.0 mg
Iron	6.0 mg

BROCCOLI SOUP (F)

from 19 months

Leftover macaroni makes a good thickening agent in soups. Makes 4 cups.

INGREDIENTS

200 g broccoli florets, rinsed
1 onion, chopped
1 large carrot, sliced
1 stick celery, sliced
1½ cups chicken stock
½ cup cooked macaroni
1 cup milk

METHOD

1. Place broccoli in a small microware container with stems facing outwards. Cover. Microwave on HIGH (90–100%) for 3 minutes.
2. Place onion in a large microware container. Microwave on HIGH (90–100%) for 1 minute to soften.
3. Add carrot, celery and 1 cup stock to onion. Cover and microwave on HIGH (90–100%) for 8 minutes.
4. Purée all vegetables and macaroni with all the stock.
5. Pour into a large microware container. Add milk and stir well. The soup will probably be warm enough for infants, so remove their serve. Heat remaining soup on HIGH (90–100%) for 2 minutes.

VARIATIONS

- Cauliflower or spinach may be used in place of broccoli.
- Use 2½ cups stock and no milk for a vibrantly coloured soup.

FREEZING

- Freeze in 1-cup portions.
- DEFROST (30-35%) 1 cup for 5-7 minutes.

NUTRIENTS
(Average per cup)
Energy 506 kJ (121 kCal)

Nutrient	Amount
Protein	13.21 g
Fat	3.72 g
Carbohydrate	8.31 g
Thiamin	0.10 mg
Riboflavin	0.23 mg
Niacin	2.30 mg
Vitamin C	45.94 mg
Calcium	40.62 mg
Iron	1.22 mg

CHUNKY CHOWDER (F)

from 19 months

This thick soup is usually made from seafood but vegetables can be used, if preferred, as it has a milk base. Soup can be an excellent way of getting children to eat vegetables. Serves 4–6.

INGREDIENTS

1 onion, chopped
3 cups milk
1 cup chicken stock
500 g potato, peeled and diced
1 × 440 g can creamed corn
2 rashers bacon

METHOD

1. Place onion in a large microware container. Cover and microwave on HIGH (90–100%) for 1 minute.
2. Add milk, stock, potato and corn. Mix well.
3. Microwave on HIGH (90–100%) for 5 minutes until nearly boiling. Reduce power to MEDIUM (50–60%) and microwave for 10 minutes, stirring occasionally.
4. Remove rind from bacon and chop finely. Place between two layers of paper towel. Microwave on HIGH (90–100%) for 2 minutes. Sprinkle on soup to serve.

VARIATIONS

- Use a leek instead of onion.
- Add a can of tuna or salmon and omit bacon.
- Sprinkle with grated cheddar cheese to serve.
- Sprinkle with a little paprika or cayenne pepper for adults.
- This soup can be mashed or puréed for younger children.

POINTER

- To scald milk in your microwave oven, pour 1 cup of milk into a 2-cup ovenable glass jug and microwave on HIGH (90–100%) for 2–3 minutes. At this point, small bubbles should be forming around the edge.

NUTRIENTS
(Average per cup)
Energy 1441 kJ (343 kCal)

Nutrient	Amount
Protein	18.24 g
Fat	10.67 g
Carbohydrate	43.91 g
Thiamin	0.35 mg
Riboflavin	0.39 mg
Niacin	4.09 mg
Vitamin C	28.04 mg
Calcium	202.35 mg
Iron	1.55 mg

MINESTRONE IN MINUTES

from 19 months

There is nothing better than a minestrone, especially in cold weather. If you haven't had time to make a hearty soup from scratch, this will make a quick meal in a bowl for baby. Frozen vegetables are still highly nutritious, losing little of their vitamin or mineral content. Choose a low-salt soup as the base.

INGREDIENTS

1 × 125 g can tomato soup
½ cup water
½ cup mixed frozen vegetables
1 tablespoon cooked rice

METHOD

1. Mix all ingredients together thoroughly in a small microware container.
2. Microwave on HIGH (90–100%) for 2 minutes. Stir well. Microwave for a further 1 minute on HIGH (90–100%). Stand for 2 minutes.

VARIATION

- Use cooked macaroni or butter beans instead of rice.

POINTER

- You can defrost small portions of frozen soups faster than larger ones. One-cup portions are recommended for convenience.

NUTRIENTS
(Average per serve)
Energy 438 kJ (105 kCal)

Nutrient	Amount
Protein	3.26 g
Fat	4.28 g
Carbohydrate	13.24 g
Thiamin	0.09 mg
Riboflavin	0.11 mg
Niacin	1.40 mg
Vitamin C	17.37 mg
Calcium	37.94 mg
Iron	1.17 mg

MINI DIM SIM SOUP

from 21 months

These appetising little dumplings are readily available in the freezer section of your supermarket and liven up a home-made chicken soup. Serves 1.

INGREDIENTS

¾ cup chicken stock
1 tablespoon finely sliced celery
1 tablespoon grated carrot
2 frozen mini dim sims

METHOD

1. Place stock, celery and carrot in a small microware bowl. Microwave on HIGH (90–100%) for 2 minutes.
2. Add dim sims, cover with lid. Microwave on MEDIUM (50–60%) for 4 minutes.

VARIATIONS

- Use 1 tablespoon grated zucchini in place of carrot.
- Adults can add a dash of Tabasco or soy sauce.

FREEZING

- DEFROST (30-35%) individual frozen dim sims for 1 minute.

POINTER

- Keep quantities of home-made chicken stock in your freezer and defrost as required on HIGH (90–100%) so that this quick soup can be cooked for your family.

NUTRIENTS
(Average per serve)
Energy 1149 kJ (275 kCal)

Protein	26.49 g
Fat	12.20 g
Carbohydrate	14.77 g
Thiamin	0.12 mg
Riboflavin	0.25 mg
Niacin	4.53 mg
Vitamin C	3.52 mg
Calcium	59.63 mg
Iron	2.07 mg

QUICK QUICHE MODERNE (F)

from 19 months

Pastry-mix adds texture and shape to this high-protein meal and helps to give an even finish for the whole family to enjoy. It's a perfect way to encourage children to eat eggs and milk.

INGREDIENTS

3 rashers bacon
¾ cup pastry-mix
½ cup milk
4 eggs, lightly beaten
1 cup grated cheddar cheese
1 tablespoon chopped chives

METHOD

1. Remove rind and excess fat from bacon and chop finely. Place between two layers of paper towel. Microwave on HIGH (90–100%) for 2 minutes.
2. Mix remaining ingredients together thoroughly. Stir in bacon. Pour into a 23-cm round ovenable glass pie dish.
3. Microwave on HIGH (90–100%) in the centre of the turntable for 8 minutes, elevated on a roasting rack (or upturned saucer).
4. Stand for 5 minutes. Serve hot or cold.

VARIATIONS

- Place a layer of sliced tomato round the edge of quiche during standing time.
- Use cooked chicken or drained, canned salmon instead of bacon.
- Add a couple of chopped spring onions in place of chives.

POINTER

- To separate uncooked bacon slices, place packet in microwave and heat on HIGH (90–100%) for 20–30 seconds. Stand for 2–3 minutes, then you can peel off slices of bacon without tearing them.

NUTRIENTS
(Average per serve of 100 g)
Energy 925 kJ (221 kCal)

Nutrient	Amount
Protein	12.95 g
Fat	12.89 g
Carbohydrate	14.22 g
Thiamin	0.13 mg
Riboflavin	0.28 mg
Niacin	1.00 mg
Vitamin C	0.42 mg
Calcium	149.89 mg
Iron	1.00 mg

EGG ON TARGET

from 19 months

A quick, nutrition-packed, balanced meal for 'mums on the run'. Spread the Vegemite thinly.

INGREDIENTS
½ muffin, toasted
butter
Vegemite
1 egg
tomato sauce

METHOD
1. Place muffin on a plate, butter and spread with a little Vegemite, particularly around the edge.
2. Crack egg into a small microware bowl. Pierce yolk. Microwave on MEDIUM (50–60%) for 40 seconds.
3. Carefully slide egg out onto muffin.
4. Using a teaspoon, scoop out egg yolk. Mash with a little tomato sauce, then return into egg.

VARIATION
- Egg yolk may be mashed with Vegemite, fish paste or mayonnaise.

POINTER
- To make tomato sauce easy to pour, remove metal lid from bottle and heat on HIGH (90–100%) for 30–45 seconds.

NUTRIENTS
(Average per serve)
Energy 790 kJ (189 kCal)

Protein	13.10 g
Fat	7.55 g
Carbohydrate	17.06 g
Thiamin	0.72 mg
Riboflavin	1.05 mg
Niacin	6.49 mg
Vitamin C	2.00 mg
Calcium	79.27 mg
Iron	1.89 mg

FASTER PASTA

Small amounts of pasta can be cooked quickly in your microwave oven. However, for large quantities cook in the traditional way.

INGREDIENTS
2 cups hot tap water
½ cup coloured noodles
¼ cup grated cheddar cheese
sprinkle of poppy or sesame seeds (optional)

METHOD

1. In a small microware container, boil water: HIGH (90–100%) for approximately 2½–3 minutes.
2. Add noodles. Stir. Microwave on MEDIUM (50–60%) for 10 minutes.
3. Drain. Toss in cheese, stir until melted. Sprinkle with a few poppy seeds or toasted sesame seeds if desired.

VARIATIONS

- Add 1 tablespoon frozen peas to cooked pasta.
- Any pasta can be cooked using this method.

FREEZING

- Place 1 cup cooked pasta in a microwave-safe plastic bag and freeze.
- DEFROST (30-35%) for 1-2 minutes. Stand for 2 minutes.

POINTER

- 1 teaspoon oil added to pasta water for cooking gives pasta a glossy finish and stops it sticking together.

NUTRIENTS
(Average per serve)
Energy 1555 kJ (372 kCal)

Nutrient	Amount
Protein	18.30 g
Fat	17.45 g
Carbohydrate	35.20 g
Thiamin	0.05 mg
Riboflavin	0.28 mg
Niacin	0.65 mg
Vitamin C	0.00 mg
Calcium	395.50 mg
Iron	0.65 mg

CHEESE MACARONI

from 19 months

Pasta is a family favourite as well as a nutritious fast food, and, as a further convenience, it refrigerates and freezes well. A serve of this dish will provide your toddler with their whole day's recommended intake of calcium and phosphorus, as well as lots of zinc and riboflavin. Makes 1⅓ cups – 1 serve.

INGREDIENTS

1½ cups hot tap water
½ cup macaroni noodles
½ cup Easy Cheese Sauce (p. 146)
½ cup grated processed cheddar cheese

METHOD

1. Bring water to the boil in a small microware container on HIGH (90–100%) for approximately 3 minutes.
2. Add macaroni, stir well, cook on HIGH (90–100%) for 8–9 minutes, until noodles are cooked.
3. Drain, add cheese sauce and cheese and stir well.
4. Reheat on MEDIUM (50–60%) for 1 minute, stirring well.

VARIATIONS

- Use wholemeal pasta for a healthy change.
- Dust with sweet paprika to add colour.

FREEZING

- Freeze in single serves in small bowls.
- DEFROST (30-35%) for 4 minutes per serve.

POINTER

- Melt cheese on LOW (30-40%) or MEDIUM (50-60%) settings to avoid a rubbery texture.

NUTRIENTS
(Average per serve)
Energy 2570 kJ (614 kCal)

Protein	32.14 g
Fat	35.38 g
Carbohydrate	42.23 g
Thiamin	0.10 mg
Riboflavin	0.63 mg
Niacin	0.75 mg
Vitamin C	0.86 mg
Calcium	833.93 mg
Iron	0.89 mg

FISH CAKES *from 19 months*

Make up a few fish cakes and freeze them for busy days. They are also a handy way of using leftover cooked potatoes. Canned salmon is a great alternative source of calcium for growing bones.

INGREDIENTS
2 large potatoes
1 × 210 g can salmon, drained
juice of ½ lemon
1 tablespoon chopped fresh parsley
1 small tomato, peeled and chopped
1 cup cornflakes, crushed

METHOD

1. Prick skin of potatoes well. Place at opposite edges of the turntable. Microwave on HIGH (90–100%) for 6–7 minutes, until cooked. Stand until cool then scoop out flesh and mash.
2. Remove large bones and mash salmon. Mix potato, salmon, lemon juice, parsley and tomato together. Shape into 6 cakes, roll in cornflake crumbs, pressing crumbs on well.
3. Place 2 cakes on paper towel on the turntable and microwave on HIGH (90–100%) for 1 minute. Serve.

VARIATIONS

- Add 130 g creamed corn to mixture.
- Add ⅓ cup drained, crushed pineapple.
- Use sweet potato instead of plain.
- Use cooked white fish such as flake, with 1 tablespoon tomato sauce.
- Make up a few cakes for children, then add a few drops of Tabasco to rest of mixture for adults.

FREEZING

- Wrap single, cooked cake in plastic wrap. Label and date and freeze.
- DEFROST (30-35%) for 2 minutes per cake - put on paper towel and turn over carefully halfway through the defrost time.

POINTERS

- To skin a tomato easily, heat tomato on HIGH (90–100%) for 45 seconds (until skin splits). Stand for 2–3 minutes, then peel.
- Salmon bones are edible and a good source of calcium; mash very well with a fork.
- Cakes can be cooked in a little butter on a pre-heated browning dish, if you have one.

NUTRIENTS
(Average per cake)
Energy 515 kJ (123 kCal)

Nutrient	Amount
Protein	9.80 g
Fat	3.48 g
Carbohydrate	12.97 g
Thiamin	0.15 mg
Riboflavin	0.21 mg
Niacin	3.43 mg
Vitamin C	18.32 mg
Calcium	137.01 mg
Iron	1.51 mg

FISH FINGER TRAIN

from 19 months

Fish fingers are quick and convenient to cook in the microwave but will dry out if overcooked.

INGREDIENT
2 fish fingers, frozen

METHOD
1. Place fish fingers on pieces of white paper towel around the edge of a roasting rack.
2. Microwave on MEDIUM-HIGH (70–80%) for 1 minute.
3. For fussy fish eater, make train tracks using beans. Place two fish fingers together. Cut one in half and stack as a chimney. Use carrot slices as wheels.

VARIATION
- Serve with tomato sauce, for dipping, as finger food.

POINTERS
- To cook 1 fish finger: microwave on MEDIUM-HIGH (70–80%) for 45 seconds.
- To cook 4 fish fingers: microwave on MEDIUM-HIGH (70–80%) for 2 minutes.

NUTRIENTS
(Average per serve)
Energy 432 kJ (103 kCal)

Protein	5.34 g
Fat	5.20 g
Carbohydrate	8.79 g
Thiamin	0.03 mg
Riboflavin	0.02 mg
Niacin	0.69 mg
Vitamin C	0.00 mg
Calcium	16.10 mg
Iron	0.46 mg

FAST FISH PIE (F) *from 19 months*

A small amount of the 'fish and vegetable of the day' can be made into a tasty pie. Serves 3.

INGREDIENTS

1 large potato
250 g rockling, flake or similar boneless fish, cut into cubes
100 g asparagus or broccoli florets, rinsed
1 cup White Sauce (p. 145)
1 tablespoon finely chopped dill or the herb of your choice
milk
sprinkle of paprika

METHOD

1. Pierce potato, elevate on a roasting rack (or upturned saucer) and place off the centre of the turntable. Microwave on HIGH (90–100%) for 4–5 minutes, turning over once. Set aside to cool.
2. Place the green vegetable in a small microware container, cover and blanch on HIGH (90–100%) for 1½ minutes.
3. Place cubed fish in a medium microware container, add asparagus or broccoli and pour over herbed white sauce.
4. Cut open potato, scoop out flesh and mash together with a little milk for a creamy consistency.
5. Spread over fish mix, sprinkle with paprika and microwave, uncovered, in the centre of the turntable on HIGH (90–100%) for 5 minutes. Stand for 3 minutes before serving.

VARIATION

- Use blanched red and green capsicums, peas or corn in this pie.

POINTER

- If strong odours remain in the microwave after cooking fish or broccoli, bring a cup of water with a lemon sliced in it to the boil for a few minutes.

NUTRIENTS
(Average per serve)
Energy 991 kJ (237 kCal)

Protein	27.06 g
Fat	8.91 g
Carbohydrate	12.25 g
Thiamin	0.13 mg
Riboflavin	0.23 mg
Niacin	6.13 mg
Vitamin C	16.18 mg
Calcium	115.59 mg
Iron	0.95 mg

SATAY FISH *from 19 months*

Cooked boneless white fish is an essential part of a varied diet as fish is high in protein and vitamins. A peanut butter and yoghurt sauce broadens its appeal by adding colour and flavour.

INGREDIENTS

100 g flake fillet
¼ banana, sliced
1 tablespoon water
2 teaspoons smooth peanut butter
1 teaspoon natural yoghurt

METHOD

1. Place fish in a small microware container. Pierce flesh in several places. Top with banana slices and pour water over.
2. Cover with plastic wrap and microwave on MEDIUM-HIGH (70–80%) for 1 minute.
3. Remove fish and banana to serving plate.
4. Blend peanut butter and yoghurt into liquid in dish. Heat on MEDIUM (50–60%) for 20–30 seconds until warmed.
5. Pour over fish. Serve with vegetables or rice.

VARIATIONS

- Older children may like the addition of a mild or sweet curry paste in the sauce.
- Use coconut cream instead of yoghurt.

POINTERS

- Pierce fish fillets several times before cooking to prevent popping.
- Soften peanut butter by removing metal lid from the jar and heating on HIGH (90–100%) for 1½ minutes per 250 g.

NUTRIENTS
(Average per serve)
Energy 992 kJ (237 kCal)

Protein	34.07 g
Fat	7.21 g
Carbohydrate	8.81 g
Thiamin	0.04 mg
Riboflavin	0.14 mg
Niacin	8.51 mg
Vitamin C	4.20 mg
Calcium	26.08 mg
Iron	0.74 mg

IRISH STEW (F) *from 19 months*

This all-time family favourite can be made without waste using tender lamb fillets, or for toddlers who like to chew a bone, lean chump chops. Adding a carrot to this classic recipe gives colour with extra nutrition and flavour. Irish stew has plenty of iron and zinc for growing toddlers. Serves 4–6.

INGREDIENTS

1¾ cups chicken stock
2 medium potatoes, cubed
1 carrot, thinly sliced
1 onion, thinly sliced
500 g lamb fillet, cut into 3-cm cubes
1 bay leaf
1 tablespoon finely chopped parsley

METHOD

1. In a 4-cup ovenable jug heat chicken stock for 5 minutes on HIGH (90–100%).
2. Place cut vegetables in the lid of a large microware container and cover with plastic wrap. Blanch on HIGH (90–100%) for 5 minutes.
3. Pierce and pound lamb and place cubes in a large microware container. Add vegetables, bay leaf and parsley. Pour over hot chicken stock. Cover.
4. Place container in the centre of the turntable, microwave on HIGH (90–100%) for 5 minutes, reduce power to MEDIUM (50–60%) and microwave for 15 minutes.
5. Stir, re-cover, reduce power to DEFROST (30–35%) and microwave for 15 minutes. Meat should be skewer-soft. Stand for 5 minutes before serving.

VARIATION

- 2 tablespoons frozen peas may be added in the last 5 minutes, to produce colour for toddlers.

FREEZING

- Freeze the entire stew by leaving in the large microwave container. Place in large freezer bag. Seal, label, date and freeze.
- Defrost on MEDIUM (50-60%) for 10 minutes.

POINTER

- Blanching hard-fibred vegetables, such as carrots and potatoes, ensures they cook in the same time as the softer-fibred lamb. Hot stock speeds up the cooking time.

NUTRIENTS
(Average per serve)
Energy 949 kJ (227 kCal)

Nutrient	Amount
Protein	30.58 g
Fat	4.75 g
Carbohydrate	14.87 g
Thiamin	0.27 mg
Riboflavin	0.34 mg
Niacin	7.85 mg
Vitamin C	21.96 mg
Calcium	28.57 mg
Iron	3.05 mg

CHICKEN AND AVOCADO CREPES

from 21 months

Crepes need to be made conventionally, so cook a dozen ahead and freeze for use on busy days. The microwave makes it easy to defrost crepes as required. Avocado is a fruit packed with vitamins.

INGREDIENTS

1 tablespoon light cream cheese
2 tablespoons avocado
60 g cooked chicken, diced
2 × 15 cm diameter cooked crepes

METHOD

1. Beat cheese and avocado together well.
2. Spread over the crepes. Place chicken pieces down the centre of each. Roll up firmly.
3. Place on paper towel on the turntable. Microwave on MEDIUM (50–60%) for 30 seconds each. Stand for 1 minute.

VARIATIONS

- Add a little lemon juice or chilli sauce to cream cheese mixture.
- Add herbs or chopped spring onion with chicken.
- Chicken can be scraped or puréed for younger children.

FREEZING

- Wrap unfilled crepes individually in microwave-safe plastic wrap and freeze.
- DEFROST (30-35%) individual crepes for 45 seconds and let stand for 1-2 minutes at room temperature.

POINTER

- Soften a hard avocado in the microwave oven by heating for 2 minutes on LOW (30-40%), turning once during the heating time. Do not overheat or avocado will blacken inside.

NUTRIENTS
(Average per 2 crepes)
Energy 1545 kJ (369 kCal)

Nutrient	Amount
Protein	24.62 g
Fat	24.57 g
Carbohydrate	12.73 g
Thiamin	0.15 mg
Riboflavin	0.33 mg
Niacin	6.94 mg
Vitamin C	7.15 mg
Calcium	92.42 mg
Iron	1.19 mg

BAKED BEAN BURGERS

from 20 months

Beans are an excellent source of protein but are not recommended for babies under twelve months as they may cause wind. For older children beans can be a useful way of preventing constipation.

INGREDIENTS

500 g potatoes
1 × 220 g can baked beans
1/3 cup corn kernels
1/4 cup grated cheddar
1 × 100 g packet corn chips, crushed

METHOD

1. Prick skins of potatoes well. Arrange around the edge of the turntable and microwave on HIGH (90–100%) for 8–10 minutes until cooked. Stand until cool, then scoop out flesh.
2. Mash potato with a little sauce from the baked beans. Add beans, corn and cheese. Mix thoroughly.
3. Shape into 8 burgers and roll in corn chip crumbs.
4. Place 2 burgers on paper towel on the turntable. Microwave on HIGH (90–100%) for 1 minute.

VARIATIONS

- For younger children, use creamed corn and crushed cereal.
- For adults, add chilli sauce or chopped spring onion.

FREEZING

- Wrap single burgers in plastic wrap. Label and date and freeze.
- To defrost, place 1 burger on paper towel and DEFROST (30-35%) for 2 minutes, turning over carefully halfway through.

POINTER

- The cooking time of dried beans varies in the microwave oven because it is determined by the size of the beans; smaller beans take longer because there are more of them in a given weight.

NUTRIENTS
(Average per burger)
Energy 624 kJ (149 kCal)

Nutrient	Amount
Protein	5.65 g
Fat	5.76 g
Carbohydrate	18.60 g
Thiamin	0.10 mg
Riboflavin	0.07 mg
Niacin	0.99 mg
Vitamin C	13.36 mg
Calcium	77.12 mg
Iron	1.06 mg

GRATED VEGIE BAKE (F)

from 19 months

Grated vegetables cook quickly in the microwave and this tasty recipe is a good way of using up the tail ends of an assortment of vegetables. It also supplies lots of Vitamin A, for good eyesight, iron from the spinach and calcium from the dairy products. Makes 4 serves.

INGREDIENTS
100 g pumpkin, grated
250 g potato, peeled and grated
1 × 250 g packet frozen spinach, thawed
100 g carrot, grated
100 g cream cheese
1/3 cup milk

METHOD

1. Press pumpkin over base of a small microware container.
2. Squeeze moisture from potato and spinach and layer respectively over pumpkin. Top with carrot. Press down firmly.
3. Cover with plastic wrap and cook on HIGH (90–100%) for 6 minutes.
4. Beat cheese until smooth and add milk, mixing well. Pour over vegetables, tap dish on bench to remove air bubbles.
5. Cook on MEDIUM (50–60%) for 3 minutes. Stand, covered, for 10–15 minutes.

VARIATION

- Add herbs or spices of your choice after the potato layer, for instance, parsley, mint, mixed herbs, nutmeg or cayenne.

POINTER

- Soften 100 g cream cheese by placing on a microwave-safe plate. Heat on DEFROST (30–35%) for 1 minute, or until spreadable.

NUTRIENTS
(Average per serve)
Energy 695 kJ (166 kCal)

Nutrient	Amount
Protein	7.00 g
Fat	9.52 g
Carbohydrate	13.37 g
Thiamin	0.14 mg
Riboflavin	0.23 mg
Niacin	1.19 mg
Vitamin C	25.82 mg
Calcium	95.72 mg
Iron	2.41 mg

FRIED RICE (F) *from 19 months*

A great way of using up leftover rice from another meal and cleaning out the vegetable crisper of small amounts of unused vegies. Makes 4 serves.

INGREDIENTS
1 egg
20 g celery, diced
20 g red pepper, diced
20 g butter
2 cups cooked white rice
¼ cup frozen peas
¼ cup corn
1 teaspoon light soy sauce

METHOD

1. Beat egg well. Pour into large microware container. Microwave on HIGH (90–100%) for 45 seconds, stirring after 15 seconds, then leave to cook into a thin, flat omelette. Stand for 1 minute, then turn out.
2. Finely dice celery and red papper. Cover, microwave on HIGH (90–100%) for 45 seconds. Remove from dish.
3. Melt butter in a large microware container on HIGH (90–100%) for 30–45 seconds until hot. Add rice and toss well in butter. Microwave on HIGH (90–100%) for 2 minutes, stirring occasionally.
4. Add rest of vegetables, stir well. Microwave on HIGH (90–100%) for 1–1½ minutes, until heated through.
5. Stir in soy sauce and chopped egg.

VARIATIONS

- Brown rice can be used in place of white.
- Add cooked diced pork, bacon or chicken.
- Add sliced mushrooms, bean sprouts and chopped spring onions.

FREEZING

- Place 1 serve in a microwave-safe freezer bag, label, date and freeze.
- DEFROST (30-35%) for 1 minute. Stand for 2 minutes and then reheat.

POINTER

- Rice freezes well. Cook a quantity and freeze in family-size portions to defrost quickly and reheat on MEDIUM (50-60%) on busy days.

NUTRIENTS
(Average per serve)
Energy 808 kJ (193 kCal)

Nutrient	Amount
Protein	4.68 g
Fat	5.76 g
Carbohydrate	30.33 g
Thiamin	0.08 mg
Riboflavin	0.08 mg
Niacin	0.99 mg
Vitamin C	10.69 mg
Calcium	14.22 mg
Iron	0.73 mg

HOME-MADE BAKED BEANS

from 19 months

There are many varieties of dried beans to choose from and they go well with other grains, meats or eggs to make a nutritious and economical meal. The high iron content of beans is made more available if eaten with a source of Vitamin C, for instance fresh fruit, at the same meal. Makes about 2 cups.

INGREDIENTS

½ cup red kidney beans
2½ cups water
¼ cup Real Tomato Sauce (p. 150)
2 teaspoons cornflour

METHOD

1. Place kidney beans with ½ cup water in a glass ovenable jug. Cover and microwave on HIGH (90–100%) for 2½ minutes or until boiling.
2. Stand for 1 hour, covered. Beans will nearly double in size.
3. Drain beans. Add another 1½ cups water to beans. Cover, microwave on HIGH (90–100%) for 5 minutes or until boiling.
4. Reduce power to LOW (30–40%) and cook for 20 minutes.
5. Mix beans with tomato sauce and microwave on HIGH (90–100%) for 1 minute. Set aside.
6. Blend cornflour with a little water to dissolve. Add remaining ½ cup water and stir. Microwave on HIGH (90–100%) for 45–60 seconds, stirring regularly until thickened.
7. Stir in tomato and bean mixture. Serve on a slice of toast or muffin.

VARIATION

- If navy or lima beans are available you can use them.

POINTER

- Speed up the preparation of all pulses (to avoid soaking them overnight) by covering with cold water, bringing to the boil on HIGH (90–100%) for about 10 minutes, then simmering on DEFROST (30–35%) for 40–45 minutes.

NUTRIENTS
(Average per ½ cup)
Energy 462 kJ (110 kCal)

Nutrient	Amount
Protein	8.01 g
Fat	1.04 g
Carbohydrate	16.43 g
Thiamin	0.17 mg
Riboflavin	0.08 mg
Niacin	1.51 mg
Vitamin C	18.07 mg
Calcium	43.90 mg
Iron	2.04 mg

CAULIFLOWER AU GRATIN (F)

from 19 months

This family favourite can be interchanged with broccoli as both are closely related members of the same family. Like broccoli, cauliflower is rich in Vitamin C and folate and provides iron and dietary fibre. The sauce supplies calcium. Serves 4.

INGREDIENTS

300 g cauliflower
20 g butter
1 tablespoon flour
½ cup milk
2 teaspoons dried breadcrumbs
1 tablespoon finely grated cheddar cheese

METHOD

1. Cut cauliflower into equal pieces. Rinse and place in a small microware container. Cover.
2. Microwave on HIGH (90–100%) for 4 minutes (or 5 minutes for very soft texture). Keep covered while making sauce.
3. Melt butter in a small microware bowl or jug on HIGH (90–100%) for 45 seconds.
4. Add flour, stir well. Microwave on HIGH (90–100%) for 30 seconds.
5. Add milk, stir well. Microwave on HIGH (90–100%) for 2 minutes, stirring well every 20 seconds until thick and smooth.
6. Pour over cauliflower. Sprinkle with breadcrumbs and cheese. Reheat for 1 minute on HIGH (90–100%).

VARIATIONS

- Use 2 teaspoons grated parmesan instead of cheddar.
- Sprinkle with paprika.
- Use broccoli in place of cauliflower, or a mixture of both.

POINTER

- Breadcrumbs can be dried by scattering 1½–2 cups fresh crumbs onto a paper-lined microwave-safe dinner plate and cooking on HIGH (90–100%) for 2–3 minutes. Stir several times to prevent burning. Cook in 1-minute bursts and check regularly.

NUTRIENTS
(Average per serve)
Energy 459 kJ (110 kCal)

Nutrient	Amount
Protein	4.75 g
Fat	7.46 g
Carbohydrate	5.63 g
Thiamin	0.08 mg
Riboflavin	0.16 mg
Niacin	0.42 mg
Vitamin C	42.32 mg
Calcium	98.59 mg
Iron	0.56 mg

STRAWBERRY AND APPLE CREPES

from 19 months

Fresh strawberries make a colourful filling for a dessert crepe.

INGREDIENTS

1 × 140 g tub strawberry and apple purée
3 tablespoons smooth ricotta cheese
1 egg, lightly beaten
6 × 15 cm diameter cooked crepes

METHOD

1. Blend fruit purée, ricotta and egg together thoroughly in a small microware container.
2. Microwave on HIGH (90–100%) for 1 minute, stirring well.
3. Microwave on LOW (30–40%) in the centre of the turntable for 3½–4 minutes, until set.
4. Stand for 5 minutes. Drain off any excess moisture.
5. Spread on crepes and roll up. Serve warm or chilled.

VARIATIONS

- Use apple purée only and place slices of strawberry down the centre of the crepe before rolling up.
- Add sultanas before rolling up.
- Filling mixture may be chilled and served as a dessert.

POINTER

- Rewarming is always done on MEDIUM (50–60%) to prevent overcooking food.

NUTRIENTS
(Average per crepe)
Energy 239 kJ (57 kCal)

Nutrient	Amount
Protein	3.35 g
Fat	2.22 g
Carbohydrate	6.04 g
Thiamin	0.03 mg
Riboflavin	0.09 mg
Niacin	0.16 mg
Vitamin C	2.92 mg
Calcium	43.75 mg
Iron	0.31 mg

BREAD AND BUTTER PUDDING (F)

from 19 months

Raisin bread makes a tasty classic pudding for the whole family to enjoy. Serves 4–6.

INGREDIENTS

5 slices of stale raisin bread, spread with jam of choice
3 × 61 g eggs at room temperature
300 ml milk at room temperature
20 g castor sugar
1 teaspoon vanilla essence
sprinkle of cinnamon

METHOD

1. Cut the bread slices into quarters and place in layers in the base of a large microware container.
2. In a 4-cup ovenable jug, whisk together the eggs, milk, sugar and vanilla. Pour over the bread and dust with cinnamon.
3. Cover and microwave off the centre of the turntable on HIGH (90–100%) for 8–10 minutes, moving the dish from one side of the turntable to the other halfway through cooking time.
4. Stand for 1–2 minutes before serving.

VARIATION

- Use stale white or brown bread instead of raisin bread, or sliced croissants.

POINTERS

- Stale bread is best for this pudding.
- Milk and eggs should be at room temperature to ensure the custard sets.

NUTRIENTS
(Average per serve)
Energy 1125 kJ (269 kCal)

Nutrient	Amount
Protein	11.83 g
Fat	9.17 g
Carbohydrate	35.38 g
Thiamin	0.12 mg
Riboflavin	0.36 mg
Niacin	0.54 mg
Vitamin C	1.20 mg
Calcium	130.91 mg
Iron	1.79 mg

YOGHURT MOUSSE

from 19 months

Yoghurt is a valuable food to have as part of your toddler's diet. It provides readily digestible calcium and protein, and is often tolerated by children who have difficulty digesting milk. Makes 2 cups.

INGREDIENTS

1 teaspoon gelatine
2 teaspoons water
100 g marshmallows
2 × 200 g tubs fruit yoghurt

METHOD

1. Mix gelatine with water in a large bowl. Cover with marshmallows.
2. Microwave on HIGH (90–100%) for 40 seconds. Marshmallows will have puffed up. Stir well to combine melted marshmallows and gelatine.
3. Add yoghurt, stir well. Marshmallows will reset in places.
4. Microwave on HIGH (90–100%) for 30–40 seconds, stirring well to remelt marshmallows and mix thoroughly.
5. Chill to set.

VARIATIONS

- Any flavoured yoghurt may be used.
- Pink marshmallows can be used with berry-flavoured yoghurt.

FREEZING

- Freeze in ice-cube trays as a treat on hot days.

POINTERS

- Fun for kids: place a few marshmallows in the microwave, heat on HIGH (90–100%) for 2–3 minutes and watch them grow huge – but don't eat them!
- Fruit yoghurt freezes excellently.

NUTRIENTS
(Average per ½ cup)
Energy 668 kJ (160 kCal)

Protein	4.99 g
Fat	2.18 g
Carbohydrate	30.18 g
Thiamin	0.10 mg
Riboflavin	0.23 mg
Niacin	0.00 mg
Vitamin C	0.00 mg
Calcium	130.83 mg
Iron	0.38 mg

Two years and on

Your child should now be taking part in family meals and dishes. However, there will be times when you only want to cook for him or her, and the following recipes give you a selection of interesting dishes to whet the appetite.

Two-year-olds are learning to be independent. This may extend to being difficult about food and refusing to eat meals you prepare. You can't force a child to eat, but if they are having fun with a meal they are more likely to eat it up. That's the time to try Vegetable Critters (p. 137–8) or Polenta People (p. 135)!

HEARTY MINESTRONE (F)

from 2 years

This soup really is a meal, and can be made quickly by using up refrigerated vegetables. Serves 4–6.

INGREDIENTS

1 medium carrot, cut into rounds
1 tablespoon light olive oil
1 brown onion, finely sliced
1 rasher bacon, roughly chopped
2 sticks celery, chopped
1 cup shredded cabbage (optional)
1 × 425 g can tomato purée
1 × 225 g can alphabet noodles

METHOD

1. Soften carrots in lid of a large microware container for 2 minutes on HIGH (90–100%).
2. Place oil and onion in the base of a large container and microwave on HIGH (90–100%) for 2½ minutes.
3. Add bacon, cook on HIGH (90–100%) for 1 minute.
4. Stir in celery, carrot and cabbage, mix well. Microwave on HIGH (90–100%) for 2½ minutes. Cover and set aside.
5. Pour tomato purée into a 6-cup ovenable glass jug, add water to make 4 cups and microwave on HIGH (90–100%) for 5 minutes.
6. Stir in noodles, cook on HIGH (90–100%) for 2 minutes to warm through.
7. Pour tomato mix on vegetables, cover and reheat soup on HIGH (90–100%) for 2–3 minutes, stirring once. Serve dusted with parmesan cheese.

VARIATION

- Add a 225 g can of mixed beans to minestrone, if desired.

FREEZING

- Place 3 cups minestrone in clean 1-litre milk carton, seal and freeze.
- To defrost, microwave on HIGH (90–100%) for 5–7 minutes.

POINTER

- Blanching fibrous vegetables before adding them to soups shortens the microwave cooking time.

NUTRIENTS
(Average per serve)
Energy 908 kJ (217 kCal)

Nutrient	Amount
Protein	11.09 g
Fat	5.93 g
Carbohydrate	30.29 g
Thiamin	0.44 mg
Riboflavin	0.24 mg
Niacin	5.27 mg
Vitamin C	122.24 mg
Calcium	90.68 mg
Iron	6.15 mg

KIDDIE PIZZA *from 2 years*

Pizzas are an all-time favourite with all age groups; here's an instant version for your toddler.

INGREDIENTS

½ muffin, toasted
2 teaspoons tomato sauce
¼ cup grated cheddar or mozzarella cheese
½ slice ham
2–3 pineapple pieces, chopped

METHOD

1. Spread toasted muffin with sauce and sprinkle with cheese.
2. Cut ham in strips or squares. Sprinkle on top of cheese and finish with pineapple.
3. Place muffin on a piece of white paper towel. Microwave on MEDIUM (50–60%) for 20–30 seconds or until cheese melts.

VARIATIONS

- Use bacon, strasbourg, devon, chicken or chopped leftover sausage.
- Use vegetable of choice, e.g. corn kernels, red and green capsicums or mushrooms.
- Use small pitta bread instead of muffins.

POINTER

- Snack foods can be successfully warmed or reheated on actual serving dishes to save cleaning up. Make sure dishes are microwave-safe and do not have gold or silver trim that may cause arcing.

NUTRIENTS
(Average per serve)
Energy 976 kJ (233 kCal)

Protein	14.17 g
Fat	11.11 g
Carbohydrate	19.23 g
Thiamin	0.19 mg
Riboflavin	0.24 mg
Niacin	1.54 mg
Vitamin C	5.33 mg
Calcium	288.87 mg
Iron	0.88 mg

MANGO FISH (F) *from 2 years*

Fruit gives colour and flavour to everyday fish fillets and also adds loads of vitamins A and C to this dish. Serves 4.

INGREDIENTS
400 g flake fillets
1 stick celery, sliced
1 mango, peeled and sliced
½ cup water
juice of ½ lemon
2 tablespoons cornflour

METHOD
1. Cut fish into even-size portions. Put in medium microwave container. Top with celery and mango, pour water and lemon juice over.
2. Cover, microwave on MEDIUM (50–60%) for 6 minutes, rotating fish once during cooking.
3. Remove fish, celery and 1 slice of mango per fillet to a serving plate. Mash remaining mango into liquid.
4. Blend cornflour with a little water to dissolve. Add to liquid, stir well.
5. Microwave on HIGH (90–100%) for 1–1½ minutes, stirring until thickened. Pour sauce over fish.

VARIATIONS
- Canned peaches can be used if mangoes are out of season.
- Add dill, parsley or other herbs to stock when cooking, and diced red capsicum for more adventurous children.

POINTERS
- Take the chill out of refrigerated fruit by heating on HIGH (90–100%) for 1–2 minutes.
- Blanch celery for 1 minute on HIGH (90–100%) before adding to this recipe.

NUTRIENTS
(Average per serve)
Energy 692 kJ (165 kCal)

Protein	30.72 g
Fat	0.30 g
Carbohydrate	9.39 g
Thiamin	0.01 mg
Riboflavin	0.09 mg
Niacin	6.77 mg
Vitamin C	13.11 mg
Calcium	13.19 mg
Iron	0.54 mg

TUNA BOATS *from 2 years*

This recipe will help your child learn about a greater variety of foods and will appeal to the finicky eater. A balanced, truly healthy dish, high in carbohydrate, with protein and minerals from the fish, and vitamins from the vegetables. Makes 4 boats.

INGREDIENTS

2 baked potatoes, cooled
½ cup milk
1 × 90 g can tuna, drained
½ cup frozen peas
2 slices cheddar cheese

METHOD

1. Cut each potato in half lengthwise. Carefully scoop out cooked pulp. Set empty shells on a microware roasting rack or microwave-safe plate.
2. Place pulp in a bowl and fork or mash into pieces. Add milk, stirring in well. Fold in tuna and peas.
3. Fill potato shells with pulp mixture (shells will be very full). Cover with paper towel and microwave on MEDIUM-HIGH (70–80%) for 6–7 minutes.
4. Diagonally cut each slice of cheese into 4 pieces (triangles) and place each triangle on a toothpick to make the sails. Before serving, place 2 sails on each potato boat.

VARIATION

- Replace tuna with cooked chicken or lamb leftovers.

FREEZING

- Place filled potatoes without sails in a microwave-safe freezer bag, label, date and freeze.
- DEFROST (30-35%) for 2 minutes per boat.

POINTER

- Jacket potatoes can be cooked in advance in the microwave and stored in the refrigerator until required.

NUTRIENTS
(Average per boat)
Energy 630 kJ (151 kCal)

Nutrient	Amount
Protein	11.91 g
Fat	5.40 g
Carbohydrate	13.28 g
Thiamin	0.12 mg
Riboflavin	0.16 mg
Niacin	3.11 mg
Vitamin C	19.77 mg
Calcium	126.95 mg
Iron	1.66 mg

KID'S CHICKEN À LA KING

from 2 years

Use up the cooked chicken and vegies from your chicken stock by creating a junior version of this popular dish. As well as protein, chicken contains lots of niacin, which is important for healthy skin and nerve development.

INGREDIENTS

From Chicken Stock recipe, p. 38:

1/3 cup stock
50 g diced cooked chicken
1 tablespoon cooked chopped celery

2 teaspoons cornflour
1 tablespoon frozen peas
2 mushrooms, chopped (optional)

METHOD

1. Blend cornflour with a little stock to dissolve.
2. Bring remaining stock to the boil in a small microware container for 1 minute on HIGH (90–100%).
3. Add cornflour paste, stir well. Microwave on HIGH (90–100%) for 45–60 seconds, stirring regularly until thickened.
4. Add remaining ingredients and heat on HIGH (90–100%) for 1–1½ minutes. Serve with rice.

VARIATION

- Replace cooked chicken with cooked fish.

POINTER

- Fresh peas can be purchased shelled if preferred.

NUTRIENTS
(Average per serve)
Energy 458 kJ (109 kCal)

Protein	11.96 g
Fat	4.08 g
Carbohydrate	6.14 g
Thiamin	0.07 mg
Riboflavin	0.21 mg
Niacin	2.73 mg
Vitamin C	2.63 mg
Calcium	12.92 mg
Iron	0.71 mg

ORANGE CHICKEN (F)

from 2 years

Skinless chicken has a mild flavour and smooth texture which can be enjoyed by the whole family. Chicken blends well with vegetables or fruit. The sweet potato provides vitamins A, C, E, thiamin and folate. Serves 4.

INGREDIENTS

4 pieces of chicken (approx. 600 g), skin removed
1 cup chicken stock
1 onion, chopped
1 orange
few black peppercorns
1 sweet potato (200 g)
2 tablespoons cornflour
sprinkle of paprika

METHOD

1. Place chicken, stock and onion in a large microware container.
2. Using a vegetable peeler, cut 3 strips of rind (without pith) from the orange. Add to stock together with peppercorns. Cover, cook on HIGH (90–100%) for 5 minutes.
3. Rotate chicken and add peeled and sliced potato.
4. Cover, cook on MEDIUM-HIGH (70–80%) for 7–10 minutes, until chicken is cooked through.
5. Remove chicken to serving plates. Strain liquid, discard peppercorns and orange rind.
6. Blend cornflour with a little orange juice to dissolve. Add to stock, stir well. Cook on HIGH (90–100%) for 1½–2 minutes, stirring regularly until thickened.
7. Return vegetables to sauce, pour over chicken and sprinkle with a little paprika to serve.

POINTERS

- Weigh chicken after the skin has been removed, so you can calculate the cooking time more accurately.
- Juice from the orange used in this recipe can be added to custard sauce.

NUTRIENTS
(Average per serve)
Energy 1285 kJ (307 kCal)

Nutrient	Amount
Protein	42.44 g
Fat	8.10 g
Carbohydrate	15.68 g
Thiamin	0.14 mg
Riboflavin	0.25 mg
Niacin	12.47 mg
Vitamin C	33.41 mg
Calcium	44.23 mg
Iron	1.49 mg

CHICKEN PIE (F) *from 2 years*

Leftover rice is handy as it makes an easy crust for a family pie. This recipe is much lower in fat and higher in carbohydrate than traditional bought pies. Serves 4.

INGREDIENTS
2 cups cooked rice
1 egg, lightly beaten
250 g boneless chicken, diced
100 g mushrooms, chopped (or baby champignons)
1 zucchini, sliced
1 × 310 g can tomato soup, lukewarm

METHOD
1. Mix rice with egg thoroughly. Press firmly over base of large microware container.
2. Cover evenly with chicken and mushrooms. Top with zucchini.
3. Pour soup over vegetables.
4. Microwave on HIGH (90–100%) for 10 minutes.
5. Stand for 5 minutes. Slice and serve.

VARIATION
- Any vegetables may be added, for instance celery, broccoli florets, diced carrot.

POINTER
- To cook 250 g skinless chicken breasts quickly in the microwave oven, elevate on a roasting rack (or upturned dinner plate), cover loosely with microwave-safe plastic wrap and cook on HIGH (90–100%) for 3½–4 minutes. Stand for 2 minutes, then use, as desired, in soups, stews or salads.

NUTRIENTS
(Average per serve)
Energy 1214 kJ (290 kCal)

Nutrient	Amount
Protein	23.91 g
Fat	7.15 g
Carbohydrate	31.82 g
Thiamin	0.12 mg
Riboflavin	0.28 mg
Niacin	7.50 mg
Vitamin C	8.39 mg
Calcium	34.84 mg
Iron	1.37 mg

CHICKEN BOATS *from 2 years*

Flat pitta bread cooks well in the microwave and provides an easy shell to fill with a tasty variety of foods.

INGREDIENTS
1 × 15 cm diameter pitta bread
½ cup mashed pumpkin
50 g cooked chicken, diced
30 g processed cheddar cheese, grated
1 teaspoon chopped parsley

METHOD
1. Split pitta in half to give two rounds. Gently press one half into a small microware rounded bowl.
2. Elevate on a roasting rack (or upturned saucer). Microwave on HIGH (90–100%) for 1¼–1½ minutes. Bread will be dry and hold its shape. Turn out to cool. Leave upturned so base dries.
3. Mix pumpkin, chicken and cheese together. Spoon into pitta shell. Sprinkle with parsley.
4. Elevate on a roasting rack (or upturned saucer) and microwave on HIGH (90–100%) for 1 minute.

VARIATIONS
- Add any cooked, leftover vegetables, e.g. corn, peas, carrots.
- Use potato instead of pumpkin.

POINTERS
- When pitta splits, one half is usually thicker. Use the thicker half and elevate for this recipe to prevent edges burning.
- Dry pitta bread in the microwave oven by splitting in half, placing both halves on white paper towel and microwaving on HIGH (90–100%) for 1½–2 minutes, turning over once. Cut into wedges and use with Chick Pea Dipper (p. 179).

NUTRIENTS
(Average per serve)
Energy 1747 kJ (417 kCal)

Protein	30.26 g
Fat	14.78 g
Carbohydrate	40.61 g
Thiamin	0.27 mg
Riboflavin	0.37 mg
Niacin	5.94 mg
Vitamin C	9.25 mg
Calcium	280.95 mg
Iron	1.97 mg

CHICKEN CANTALOUP SALAD

from 2 years

This juicy melon is a great addition to a salad in summer.

INGREDIENTS

150 g cantaloup, diced
½ teaspoon honey
1 tablespoon light cream cheese or natural yoghurt
1 cooked chicken fillet, diced
½ cup cooked coloured noodles (see p. 96)

METHOD

1. Place 50 g of melon in a small microware bowl. Cover. Microwave on HIGH (90–100%) for 30 seconds.
2. Purée cooked cantaloup with honey and cream cheese or yoghurt to make a dressing. Chill.
3. Toss remaining cantaloup with chicken and noodles. Pour over dressing and serve.

VARIATION

- Add chopped chives or celery to salad.

POINTER

- Soften crystallised honey by removing metal lid from the jar and heating hardened honey on HIGH (90–100%) for 30 seconds. Stir until honey is smooth.

NUTRIENTS
(Average per serve)
Energy 1741 kJ (416 kCal)

Nutrient	Amount
Protein	50.33 g
Fat	9.32 g
Carbohydrate	31.91 g
Thiamin	0.16 mg
Riboflavin	0.33 mg
Niacin	14.43 mg
Vitamin C	27.00 mg
Calcium	128.10 mg
Iron	1.71 mg

MINTED LAMB *from 2 years*

Lamb fillet makes a lean cuisine for a toddler without much fuss. If unavailable, ask the butcher for boned, trimmed loin.

INGREDIENTS

1 lamb fillet (about 60 g)
1 tablespoon natural yoghurt
2 mint leaves, chopped (or 1 teaspoon mint jelly)

METHOD

1. Flatten lamb with a meat mallet and cut into strips.
2. Thread meat on 2 wooden skewers.
3. Mix yoghurt and mint leaves together. Pour over meat and marinate for 2 hours.
4. Microwave lamb stick on MEDIUM-HIGH (70–80%) for 80–90 seconds.
5. Remove sticks. Serve with vegetables or on pitta bread with lettuce and tomato.

VARIATION

- Use chicken fillet in place of lamb fillet.

POINTER

- Piercing and pounding meat, as well as cutting it into strips, results in a more tender meal for your child.

NUTRIENTS
(Average per serve)
Energy 390 kJ (93 kCal)

Protein	14.53 g
Fat	3.22 g
Carbohydrate	1.13 g
Thiamin	0.10 mg
Riboflavin	0.22 mg
Niacin	3.00 mg
Vitamin C	0.00 mg
Calcium	50.40 mg
Iron	1.08 mg

LEMON VEAL (F) *from 2 years*

The white, tender and delicate meat of baby veal goes perfectly with the acid taste of lemon juice, especially on warm days. Rich in iron, zinc and vitamins A and C. Serves 4.

INGREDIENTS
100 g carrot
200 g zucchini
350 g veal schnitzel
1 tablespoon cornflour
½ cup chicken stock
juice of small lemon
1 tablespoon chopped parsley

METHOD

1. Cut vegetables into matchsticks or thin slices. Cut veal into strips.
2. Place carrots in a large microware container. Cover, microwave on HIGH (90–100%) for 1 minute.
3. Add zucchini. Cover, microwave on HIGH (90–100%) for 1 minute.
4. Remove vegetables. Place meat in container and microwave on HIGH (90–100%) for 2 minutes, stirring occasionally.
5. Add vegetables. Cover and stand while making sauce.
6. Blend cornflour with a little stock to dissolve. Add remaining stock and lemon juice. Stir well. Microwave on HIGH (90–100%) for 1½–2 minutes, stirring regularly until thickened.
7. Add parsley to sauce. Pour over meat and vegetables. Stir well. Serve with rice.

VARIATIONS

- Pork schnitzels can be used in place of veal.
- Other vegetables may be added. For children who like crunchy vegetables, halve their cooking times.

POINTER

- Blanching vegetables before adding to casseroles ensures they cook evenly and in the same time as the meat.

NUTRIENTS
(Average per serve)
Energy 497 kJ (119 kCal)

Protein	21.05 g
Fat	1.51 g
Carbohydrate	4.69 g
Thiamin	0.16 mg
Riboflavin	0.27 mg
Niacin	4.47 mg
Vitamin C	17.54 mg
Calcium	24.02 mg
Iron	1.80 mg

SHEPHERD'S PIE (F) *from 2 years*

An old-fashioned family favourite that can be made either with beef or lamb mince. Serves 4.

INGREDIENTS
400 g potatoes, peeled and cubed
milk
1 onion, finely chopped
500 g minced beef or lamb
1/3 cup fresh peas, shelled
1/4 cup beef or vegetable stock
3 teaspoons gravy flour
Worcestershire sauce and pepper

METHOD

1. Microwave potatoes on HIGH (90-100%) for 6–7 minutes, until cooked. Mash with a little milk and set aside.
2. Place onion in a medium microware container. Cover, microwave on HIGH (90–100%) for 1 minute to soften.
3. Add meat. Cook on HIGH (90–100%) for 3 minutes until browned, stirring several times.
4. Add peas and stock. Cover, microwave on MEDIUM (50–60%) for 10 minutes, stirring occasionally.
5. Blend gravy flour with a little water to dissolve. Add to meat, stir thoroughly. Microwave on MEDIUM (50–60%) for 1 minute, stirring well.
6. Remove child's portion to serving plate and top with some mashed potato.
7. Add Worcestershire sauce and pepper to adult meat. Stir well. Top with mashed potato. Microwave on MEDIUM (50–60%) for 4–5 minutes, until potato is warm.

VARIATIONS

- Sprinkle with grated cheddar cheese on removal from oven when finished cooking.
- The pie can quickly be browned under a hot grill.

FREEZING

- Freeze in single serve portions (approximately 200 g).
- DEFROST (30-35%) for 4-5 minutes.

POINTERS

- Baby potatoes (75 g or less) are best peeled, cut and covered for cooking when they are to be mashed. A squeeze of lemon juice prevents blackening.
- Stir mince meat frequently when cooking to break it up and prevent lumpiness.

NUTRIENTS
(Average per serve)
Energy 1311 kJ (313 kCal)

Nutrient	Amount
Protein	43.12 g
Fat	8.08 g
Carbohydrate	16.54 g
Thiamin	0.30 mg
Riboflavin	0.49 mg
Niacin	8.65 mg
Vitamin C	24.11 mg
Calcium	22.84 mg
Iron	4.69 mg

BEEF STICK-UP *from 2 years*

Satays offer manageable pieces of meat for toddlers to munch. This is a favourite of Jack's and his friends. Serves 4 children.

INGREDIENTS
300 g beef schnitzel (uncrumbed)
1 sachet instant soup (beef, beef and vegetables or vegetable)
1/4 cup water
1 tablespoon tomato sauce
1 teaspoon light soy sauce

METHOD
1. Cut beef into 1-cm thick strips.
2. Mix remaining ingredients together thoroughly in a small container. Add meat, stir well to coat strips. Marinate for a minimum of 2 hours.
3. Thread meat on 8 wooden satay sticks.
4. Arrange 4 satay sticks around the edge of the turntable. Spoon a little marinade over each stick.
5. Microwave on HIGH (90–100%) for 2 minutes. Repeat to cook remainder. Serve with rice, pasta or vegetables.

VARIATION
- Use lamb or chicken with a soup to match.

FREEZING
- Wrap 2 cooked 'stick-ups' in microwave-safe plastic wrap and freeze.
- DEFROST (30-35%) for 1 minute, turning once.

POINTERS
- Use a meat mallet to flatten and tenderise beef.
- Marinating meat flavours and tenderises for quick microwave cooking.

NUTRIENTS
(Average per 2 satays)
Energy 482 kJ (115 kCal)

Nutrient	Amount
Protein	16.87 g
Fat	3.94 g
Carbohydrate	2.93 g
Thiamin	0.12 mg
Riboflavin	0.20 mg
Niacin	3.51 mg
Vitamin C	1.38 mg
Calcium	11.63 mg
Iron	2.86 mg

PORK HOT POT (F) *from 2 years*

New-fashioned cuts of pork are lean, low-fat and easy to digest. Pork adapts well to delicious meals in one with vegetables, pasta or rice. It is also very rich in thiamin. Serves 4.

INGREDIENTS

1 carrot, sliced
1 small parsnip, sliced
1 stick celery, sliced
1 cup water
500 g pork (schnitzel or butterfly steaks), cut into 2-cm cubes
2 tablespoons cornflour
1–3 tablespoons plum sauce

METHOD

1. Place vegetables and water in a large microware container. Microwave on HIGH (90–100%) for 5 minutes.
2. Add meat. Cover, microwave on MEDIUM (50–60%) for 10 minutes, stirring occasionally.
3. Blend flour with some water to form a smooth paste. Add to casserole and stir very well. Cook, uncovered, for 1–2 minutes on MEDIUM (50–60%) until thickened.
4. Stir in plum sauce to taste and serve with rice, garnished with spring onions, if desired.

VARIATIONS

- Beef or chicken stock can be used in place of water.
- Add 100 g blanched snow peas to garnish.

FREEZING

- Freeze in single-serve portions (approx. 250 g).
- DEFROST (30-35%) for 5 minutes per portion.

POINTER

- Piercing and pounding casserole meat lightly helps tenderise it for microwave cooking.

NUTRIENTS
(Average per serve)
Energy 691 kJ (165 kCal)

Nutrient	Amount
Protein	26.26 g
Fat	1.91 g
Carbohydrate	10.42 g
Thiamin	0.84 mg
Riboflavin	0.30 mg
Niacin	5.88 mg
Vitamin C	4.13 mg
Calcium	34.88 mg
Iron	1.38 mg

PORK AND APPLE MEAT LOAF (F)

from 2 years

Versatile, lean pork mince bakes well in the microwave as well as being suitable for traditional burgers or baby bite-size pork balls. Meat loaf can be used as a sandwich filling for toddlers. Serves 4–5.

INGREDIENTS

500 g pork mince
1 egg, lightly beaten
1 cup fresh breadcrumbs
1 carrot, grated
1 apple, peeled and grated
1 tablespoon chopped chives

METHOD

1. Mix pork, egg, breadcrumbs and carrot together thoroughly.
2. Squeeze excess moisture from apple. Add apple and chives to meat and mix well.
3. Press into a microwave ring pan. Cook on HIGH (90–100%) for 6–7 minutes.
4. Stand for 5 minutes before serving.

VARIATIONS

- Sprinkle with grated cheddar or toasted coconut to serve.
- Add chopped dried prunes or apricots to mixture.
- Excess apple juice may be added to a gravy to serve with meat loaf.

POINTER

- Using a microware cake-ring container to cook meat loaves ensures microwaves penetrate evenly to heat the food within quickly. Elevating container allows microwaves to penetrate from below.

NUTRIENTS
(Average per serve)
Energy 1362 kJ (325 kCal)

Nutrient	Amount
Protein	31.53 g
Fat	12.06 g
Carbohydrate	22.64 g
Thiamin	0.92 mg
Riboflavin	0.36 mg
Niacin	6.32 mg
Vitamin C	3.95 mg
Calcium	42.60 mg
Iron	2.06 mg

MAKE-BELIEVE HOT DOG

from 2 years

Make the most of leftovers with a crepe dog. You can keep pre-cooked crepes in the freezer and defrost as required for a quick snack, meal or dessert.

INGREDIENTS

1 × 15 cm diameter crepe
¼ cup mashed potato
1–2 teaspoons tomato sauce
1 cooked sausage, skin removed

METHOD

1. Spread mashed potato over crepe.
2. Place sausage in the middle and top with tomato sauce.
3. Wrap firmly. Cover with baking paper.
4. Microwave on MEDIUM (50–60%) for 2 minutes.

VARIATIONS

- Add some creamed corn to the potato.
- Use mustard, pickle or chutney instead of tomato sauce.
- Any flavoured sausage can be used.

FREEZING

- Layer crepes with plastic wrap between them.
- DEFROST (30-35%) individual crepes for 45 seconds. Stand for 1-2 minutes at room temperature.

POINTER

- Mashed potato reheats quickly in the microwave in small amounts. Depress the centre for best results.

NUTRIENTS
(Average per serve)
Energy 1227 kJ (293 kCal)

Nutrient	Amount
Protein	13.99 g
Fat	15.74 g
Carbohydrate	23.73 g
Thiamin	0.07 mg
Riboflavin	0.20 mg
Niacin	5.03 mg
Vitamin C	8.61 mg
Calcium	90.26 mg
Iron	1.82 mg

HAMBURGERS (F) *from 2 years*

Fat-free and fast from your microwave oven, these lean hamburgers can be enjoyed by the whole family. With a wholemeal bun and salad they make a balanced meal. Makes 6 burgers.

INGREDIENTS
500 g minced beef
1 egg
¼ cup dried breadcrumbs
1 sachet dried instant soup, vegetable or tomato

METHOD
1. Mix all ingredients together thoroughly.
2. Shape into 6 burgers
3. Place on a roasting rack and cover with white paper towel. Microwave on HIGH (90–100%) for 5 minutes for 4 burgers (3 minutes for 2); turn over and rotate once during cooking. Stand for 1 minute.
4. Serve in hamburger rolls with lettuce, tomato and cheese.

VARIATION
- Add grated carrot, spring onion or herbs to mixture.

POINTERS
- Microwaved hamburgers can be darkened by adding 1 tablespoon soy sauce, Worcestershire sauce or parisian essence to the ingredients.
- Hamburgers may be two-thirds cooked in the microwave and finished off on a barbecue. Always barbecue immediately after pre-cooking in the microwave.

NUTRIENTS
(Average per burger)
Energy 766 kJ (183 kCal)

Protein	18.58 g
Fat	10.32 g
Carbohydrate	4.05 g
Thiamin	0.08 mg
Riboflavin	0.16 mg
Niacin	3.39 mg
Vitamin C	0.00 mg
Calcium	15.41 mg
Iron	2.22 mg

OATY MEAT BALLS (F)

from 2 years

Keep a packet of oats in the cupboard as it is an ingredient that can be used in many recipes. For instance, it helps to extend meats – add to meat loaves and terrines based on beef, pork or veal – and additionally it provides soluble fibre and complex carbohydrate.

INGREDIENTS

1 onion, finely chopped
500 g minced beef or lamb
1 egg, lightly beaten
1 cup instant oats
¼ teaspoon dried basil
1 × 440 g can condensed tomato soup

METHOD

1. Place onion in a large microware container. Cover, microwave on HIGH (90–100%) for 1 minute to soften.
2. Add beef and egg, mix well. Add oats and basil and mix thoroughly. Shape into 10 balls. Arrange around the edge of the large container.
3. Pour tomato soup over meat balls. Cover with lid. Microwave on HIGH (90–100%) for 10 minutes, turning meat balls several times during cooking. Serve with rice or pasta.

VARIATIONS

- Add grated carrot, corn kernels or sliced mushrooms to meat mixture.
- Beef consommé or other soups can be used in place of tomato soup.
- Add crushed garlic, Worcestershire sauce and additional herbs to adult meat mixture. A little red wine can be added to sauce for the adults. Re-warm for 2–3 minutes on MEDIUM-HIGH (70–80%). Children's meat balls can be flagged with a toothpick for identification while cooking.

FREEZING

- Place 2 balls with sauce per serve in microwave-safe plastic bags and freeze.
- DEFROST (30-35%) for 4½-5 minutes per serve.

POINTER

- Use leftover oats by adding them to soups, to thicken and enrich the flavour.

NUTRIENTS
(Average per 2 meatballs)
Energy 828 kJ (198 kCal)

Nutrient	Amount
Protein	15.24 g
Fat	10.26 g
Carbohydrate	11.16 g
Thiamin	0.14 mg
Riboflavin	0.14 mg
Niacin	2.82 mg
Vitamin C	0.70 mg
Calcium	23.88 mg
Iron	2.26 mg

HAM STEAK MATES

from 2 years

Use lean ham for this fun meal as nutritionally ham scores well; although it is salty it is a tasty way of supplying iron, zinc, magnesium and thiamin.

INGREDIENTS

1 ham steak
1 slice canned pineapple
1 small piece red capsicum or ½ cherry tomato
8 snow peas
½ cup mashed potato

METHOD

1. Place ham steak on flat microware dish. Cut pineapple slice in half. Position one half as a smile, cut the other half into pieces as eyes. Put capsicum or tomato, skin side up, as nose.
2. Cover with microwave-safe plastic wrap. Microwave on HIGH (90–100%) for 1–1½ minutes. Stand for 1 minute.
3. Top and tail snow peas. Wrap tightly in plastic wrap. Microwave on HIGH (90–100%) for 30 seconds.
4. Heat mashed potato on HIGH (90–100%) for approximately 1 minute.
5. Place ham steak on a serving plate. Place snow peas around meat as hair and mashed potato as a bow tie.

POINTER

- Small amounts of mashed potato reheat quickly. Make a depression in the centre for most efficient reheating.

NUTRIENTS
(Average per serve)
Energy 1338 kJ (320 kCal)

Nutrient	Amount
Protein	40.91 g
Fat	6.59 g
Carbohydrate	23.50 g
Thiamin	1.32 mg
Riboflavin	0.41 mg
Niacin	9.52 mg
Vitamin C	41.60 mg
Calcium	55.70 mg
Iron	2.73 mg

TOFU TOSS *from 2 years*

If your child is not keen on meat, try tofu which is soybean curd and is available from the refrigerated section of your supermarket. It is similar in appearance to baked custard, with a firm texture, and contains high-quality protein like meat.

POINTER

■ Use a MEDIUM (50–60%) power to warm or reheat tofu, to prevent it toughening.

INGREDIENTS

125 g tofu
1 tablespoon light soy sauce
2 sticks celery, cut diagonally
½ red capsicum, cut into thin strips
1 tablespoon fresh peas

METHOD

1. Put light soy sauce into base of a medium microware container and marinate tofu for 30 minutes, turning several times.
2. Microwave tofu, covered, in the centre of the turntable for 2½–3 minutes on MEDIUM (50–60%). Set aside.
3. Microwave vegetables and 1 tablespoon water in a large container on HIGH (90–100%) for 2 minutes.
4. Cut tofu into 2-cm cubes and toss together with cooked, drained vegetables. Serve with rice.

VARIATION

■ For babies under twelve months, mash and mix tofu with puréed fruit.

NUTRIENTS
(Average per serve)
Energy 589 kJ (141 kCal)

Nutrient	Amount
Protein	13.28 g
Fat	5.62 g
Carbohydrate	10.91 g
Thiamin	75.10 mg
Riboflavin	0.14 mg
Niacin	1.51 mg
Vitamin C	106.26 mg
Calcium	201.30 mg
Iron	3.85 mg

POTATO PUPS

from 2 years

If you have a small helper in the kitchen, try this really easy-to-prepare recipe. The simple kitchen clean-up should appeal to all kitchen hands. Potato is also excellent nutritionally, rich in carbohydrate, vitamins and iron.

INGREDIENTS

1 medium potato
1 frankfurt
1 tablespoon grated cheddar cheese

METHOD

1. Pierce potato in several places and elevate on a roasting rack (or upturned saucer) off the centre of the turntable.
2. Microwave on HIGH (90–100%) for 4 minutes, turning once.
3. Stand to cool, then split in half and scoop out the pulp and mash well.
4. Slice frankfurt in half lengthwise. Place in a small microwave-safe bowl. Fill with potato and top with cheese.
5. Microwave on HIGH (90–100%), until frankfurt has heated and the cheese has melted.

VARIATION

- Chicken, beef or turkey sausages can be used in this recipe also.

POINTERS

- 250 g cold cheese can be warmed in the microwave on MEDIUM (50–60%) for 30–60 seconds to make it easier to grate or slice.
- Peel skin from frankfurt for young children, to avoid choking.

NUTRIENTS
(Average per serve)
Energy 1335 kJ (319 kCal)

Nutrient	Amount
Protein	17.27 g
Fat	18.69 g
Carbohydrate	20.58 g
Thiamin	0.16 mg
Riboflavin	0.21 mg
Niacin	2.35 mg
Vitamin C	30.45 mg
Calcium	212.65 mg
Iron	1.95 mg

RISOTTO (F)

from 2 years

The microwave oven has liberated cooks from the continual stirring traditionally associated with this tasty dish. Any recipe based on rice will be a great source of carbohydrate, but this risotto includes Vitamin-A rich carrots, iron-rich zucchini and fibre-rich sweetcorn as well as calcium from the cheese! Serves 4.

INGREDIENTS

2 cups chicken stock
1/3 cup rice
50 g carrot, grated
50 g zucchini, grated
1/4 cup corn kernels
1 small tomato, chopped
1/2 cup grated cheddar cheese

METHOD

1. Bring stock to the boil in a medium microware container by heating for approximately 5 minutes on HIGH (90–100%).
2. Add rice and vegetables, stir well. Cook on HIGH (90–100%) for 15 minutes or until liquid is absorbed and rice is cooked.
3. Sprinkle cheese on top and stand for 2 minutes.

VARIATIONS

- Any vegetable may be used or you may prefer the addition of cooked chicken.
- Season with freshly ground pepper for adults.
- Use lamb or beef stock instead of chicken stock.

POINTER

- Skin a tomato easily in your microwave oven by piercing the skin lightly with a fork, elevating on a roasting rack (or upturned saucer) and heating on HIGH (90–100%) for 45 seconds. Stand for 2–3 minutes, then peel.

NUTRIENTS
(Average per serve)
Energy 658 kJ (157 kCal)

Nutrient	Amount
Protein	6.98 g
Fat	6.70 g
Carbohydrate	17.09 g
Thiamin	0.06 mg
Riboflavin	0.13 mg
Niacin	0.98 mg
Vitamin C	9.19 mg
Calcium	159.82 mg
Iron	0.46 mg

POLENTA PEOPLE *from 2 years*

Polenta is a cornmeal pudding that can be cut into wedges or diamond shapes to accompany various foods. Cutting it into shapes appeals to toddlers.

INGREDIENTS
3 cups water
1 cup polenta (cornmeal)
1/3 cup grated processed cheddar
1 tablespoon chopped parsley

METHOD

1. Bring water to the boil in a 1-litre ovenable glass jug.
2. Add polenta and stir well. Microwave on HIGH (90–100%) for 2 minutes, stirring well.
3. Cover and vent. Microwave on MEDIUM-HIGH (70–80%) for 5 minutes.
4. Stir in cheese and parsley and mix well. Pour into a pie plate and allow to cool and set.
5. Turn out onto a cutting board. Using a cutter (gingerbread man, animal or shapes), cut into various shapes and let children decorate with extra parsley, corn kernels or tomato sauce.

VARIATION

- For babies under twelve months, mash polenta with fresh puréed fruit.

POINTER

- Bring 250 g cheese to room temperature by unwrapping, placing on a microwave-safe plate and heating on MEDIUM (50–60%) for 30–40 seconds. This makes it easier to slice or grate.

NUTRIENTS
(Average per 100 g)
Energy 303 kJ (73 kCal)

Nutrient	Amount
Protein	2.50 g
Fat	1.83 g
Carbohydrate	11.32 g
Thiamin	0.10 mg
Riboflavin	0.03 mg
Niacin	0.10 mg
Vitamin C	0.21 mg
Calcium	35.12 mg
Iron	0.15 mg

TOMATO ZUCCHINI BAKE (F)

from 2 years

An easy vegetable side dish for roast dinners, grills or barbecues. Rich in vitamins A and C from the tomatoes, it also supplies calcium. Leftovers can be used as a topping on toast for a healthy snack. Serves 3–4.

INGREDIENTS

1 large tomato, sliced
1 small onion, sliced or grated
1 zucchini, chopped
½ cup processed cheddar cheese, grated
¼ cup breadcrumbs

METHOD

1. Layer tomato, onion and zucchini in a small microware container.
2. Cover, microwave on HIGH (90–100%) for 5 minutes.
3. Mix cheese and breadcrumbs together. Sprinkle over vegetables. Stand for 2–3 minutes, slice and serve.

VARIATIONS

- Use spring onion or chives for younger children.
- Sprinkle mixed herbs over the tomato.
- Add a few finely chopped sun-dried tomatoes for adult serves.

POINTER

- Grating onion when adding to dishes ensures it cooks in the time other ingredients take.

NUTRIENTS
(Average per serve)
Energy 410 kJ (98 kCal)

Nutrient	Amount
Protein	5.90 g
Fat	5.54 g
Carbohydrate	6.10 g
Thiamin	0.05 mg
Riboflavin	0.12 mg
Niacin	0.85 mg
Vitamin C	16.64 mg
Calcium	134.46 mg
Iron	0.61 mg

VEGETABLE CRITTERS

from 2 years

By the age of two many children begin to dislike some vegetables, so it takes a bit of bribery and imagination to get them back on the menu. Try these animals for fun and get the kids to help.

ELEPHANT

1 scoop mashed potato, pumpkin or carrot
2 carrot slices
2 peas
1 bean, snow pea or cheese stick

Make body of elephant from mashed potato, add ears of carrot and eyes of peas, then trunk of bean, snow pea or cheese stick.

RABBIT

1 tomato slice
2 baby carrots or celery sticks
small wedge of cheese
bean shoots or carrot sticks
2 peas
slice of celery

Make rabbit face with tomato slice. Add ears of carrot, or celery sticks 2–3 cm long. The cheese makes a nose, and the bean shoots or thin carrot sticks whiskers. Peas are the eyes, while a thin slice of celery makes the mouth.

LADYBIRD

1 scoop mashed potato, pumpkin or carrot
peas
4 thin strips cheese or beans

Make the body of potato, and add pea spots. 2 strips of cheese should be placed approximately down the middle of the back, joining towards the head but with space between them at the rear, as wing dividers. The last 2 pieces of cheese (or beans) make antennae at the head.

PORCUPINE

1 scoop mashed potato, pumpkin or carrot
grated cheddar cheese
2 oval carrot slices
end of carrot or cheese wedge

Make body out of mashed potato and scatter cheese over as spikes. The carrot slices are the feet, and the end of the carrot makes the nose.

BUTTERFLY

1 baby carrot
2 slices red or green capsicum
1 scoop mixed mashed potato and pumpkin

The body is made out of the carrot, while the edges of the wings are the capsicum slices. The wings are filled with potato and pumpkin.

SPIDER

1 scoop mashed potato, pumpkin or carrot
4 green beans
2 peas or corn kernels

The body is of mashed potato. Halve the beans and place around body as legs. Finally place 2 peas at one end of the potato body as eyes.

FRUIT MEDLEY CREPES

from 2 years

Dried fruit is rich in fibre, vitamin A, minerals and sugar, which is attractive to microwave energy, so make sure fruit is mixed thoroughly through fillings to prevent burning. These crepes make a nutrient-packed snack or dessert.

INGREDIENTS

1/2 cup chopped dried apple
1/3 cup chopped dried apricots
1 piece dried pawpaw, chopped
1/2 cup water
2 tablespoons cream cheese
4 cooked crepes (about 15 cm diameter)

METHOD

1. Place chopped fruit in a small microware container. Cover with water. Microwave on HIGH (90–100%) for 3 minutes, stirring each minute.
2. Stand for 2 minutes. Add cream cheese and mix well. Spoon some filling down the centre of each crepe. Roll up firmly.
3. Serve warm or chilled. Sprinkle with a little icing sugar or cinnamon sugar, if desired.

FREEZING

- Wrap filled crepes individually in plastic wrap and freeze.
- DEFROST (30-35%) for 1 minute and stand for 1-2 minutes at room temperature.

POINTER

- Dried fruits may be softened or plumped in your microwave oven by adding 1/4 cup liquid to 1 cup fruit, covering and heating on HIGH (90–100%) for 1-2 minutes. Stir through and allow to cool.

NUTRIENTS
(Average per crepe)
Energy 500 kJ (120 kCal)

Nutrient	Amount
Protein	3.70 g
Fat	4.56 g
Carbohydrate	16.34 g
Thiamin	0.05 mg
Riboflavin	0.12 mg
Niacin	0.64 mg
Vitamin C	20.12 mg
Calcium	54.44 mg
Iron	0.86 mg

THREE MILKS ICE CREAM (F)

from 2 years

Home-made is best, and certainly a lot cheaper than commercial brands as family fare.

INGREDIENTS

1 × 375 g can evaporated milk
1 cup milk
3 egg yolks
200 g sweetened condensed milk
1 teaspoon vanilla essence

METHOD

1. Chill open can of evaporated milk in the freezer for a couple of hours until ice crystals form around the edges.
2. Place plain milk in a small container or jug and microwave on HIGH (90–100%) for 1 minute.
3. Beat yolks well. Add warmed milk, stir thoroughly. Microwave on LOW (30–40%) for 8 minutes, stirring every 30 seconds, until mixture thickens to coat spoon.
4. Cool. Add condensed milk and vanilla. Chill.
5. Whip evaporated milk in a large bowl with electric beaters until thick, creamy and doubled in volume.
6. Add the other milk mixture and mix thoroughly. Pour into a 2-litre ice cream container and freeze for 1½–2 hours.
7. Rewhip. Freeze ready for use.

VARIATIONS

- **Chocolate** Blend 1 tablespoon cocoa with 2 tablespoons water until dissolved and no lumps. Add with the condensed milk, mixing well.
- **Rich creamy ice cream** Use 300 ml lightly whipped cream instead of evaporated milk. Whip 2 egg whites until stiff. Fold into cream after milks have been added.
- **Strawberry** Add 1 tablespoon strawberry topping with the condensed milk.

POINTER

- Egg whites can be frozen in ice-cube trays.

NUTRIENTS
(Average per 100 g)
Energy 719 kJ (172 kCal)

Protein	7.35 g
Fat	8.25 g
Carbohydrate	18.43 g
Thiamin	0.07 mg
Riboflavin	0.42 mg
Niacin	0.00 mg
Vitamin C	0.94 mg
Calcium	203.91 mg
Iron	0.39 mg

STEAMED PUMPKIN PUDDING (F)

from 2 years

This old-fashioned pud can be made in just 13 minutes in a handy ovenable glass jug without fuss, foil and string, and in less than a quarter of the conventional time. Pumpkin is rich in vitamins A and C. Serves 6.

INGREDIENTS

60 g butter or margarine
1 cup sultanas
2 tablespoons water
1¼ cups self-raising flour
1 cup lightly packed brown sugar
1 teaspoon cinnamon
½ teaspoon nutmeg
¼ teaspoon ground cloves
1 cup puréed pumpkin
1 egg, lightly beaten

METHOD

1. Place butter, sultanas and water in a small microware container. Cover, cook on HIGH (90–100%) for 2 minutes.
2. Mix flour, sugar and spices together. Stir in sultana mixture, pumpkin and egg. Stir until well mixed.
3. Pour into a greased 4-cup glass jug. Cover with plastic wrap and cook, elevated, on a roasting rack (or upturned saucer) on MEDIUM (50–60%) for 13 minutes in the centre of the turntable.
4. Keep covered, stand directly on bench for 10 minutes before turning out to serve with custard or ice cream.

VARIATION

- Raisins can be used in place of sultanas.

FREEZING

- Cut pudding in half. Cool, wrap each half well in plastic wrap, label and freeze.
- DEFROST (30-35%) for 3 minutes, turning once. Stand.

POINTERS

- You can use a ring-shaped container if you do not have a glass jug, but glass aids steaming, especially when tightly covered with plastic wrap.
- Purée a small 500 g pumpkin in its skin by piercing several times, elevating on a roasting rack and microwaving on HIGH (90-100%) for 8-10 minutes. Stand to cool, then scoop out purée, discarding seeds.

NUTRIENTS
(Average per serve)
Energy 1649 kJ (394 kCal)

Nutrient	Amount
Protein	5.08 g
Fat	9.38 g
Carbohydrate	73.07 g
Thiamin	0.11 mg
Riboflavin	0.09 mg
Niacin	0.74 mg
Vitamin C	4.81 mg
Calcium	63.00 mg
Iron	0.03 mg

PEACH SPONGE PUDDING (F)

from 2 years

A light sponge cake is ideally suited to microwave cooking as it does not need a crust and is traditionally a pale colour. Make sure the flour you use is a quality brand and the eggs fresh. Serves 4–6.

INGREDIENTS

1 × 425 g can pie peaches
2 eggs
1/3 cup brown sugar
2 tablespoons each self-raising flour, plain flour and cornflour
2 tablespoons desiccated coconut, toasted

METHOD

1. Place peaches around the base of a microware cake-ring dish.
2. Whisk eggs until thick, pale and creamy. Gradually add sugar, beating well after each addition. Gently fold in flours, mix thoroughly. Spoon evenly over peaches.
3. Sprinkle with coconut. Microwave on HIGH (90–100%) for 3½ minutes.
4. Stand for 5 minutes before serving with custard or ice cream.

VARIATION

- Use a can of pie apple instead of pie peaches.

FREEZING

- Freeze a plain sponge cake in microwave-safe plastic wrap.
- DEFROST (30-35%) for 1-1½ minutes in 10-second bursts. Stand for 20-30 minutes.

POINTER

- To toast coconut, microwave ½ cup coconut on HIGH (90–100%) for 3–4 minutes, stirring occasionally.

NUTRIENTS
(Average per serve)
Energy 858 kJ (205 kCal)

Nutrient	Amount
Protein	5.22 g
Fat	4.49 g
Carbohydrate	35.65 g
Thiamin	0.05 mg
Riboflavin	0.15 mg
Niacin	0.69 mg
Vitamin C	6.38 mg
Calcium	21.95 mg
Iron	0.98 mg

PLAYDOUGH *from 2 years*

The recipe for playdough has been around for many years but the microwave makes it without a tough saucepan to clean! Makes approximately 2 cups.

INGREDIENTS
1 cup plain flour
½ cup cooking salt
2 tablespoons cream of tartar
1 tablespoon cooking oil
1 cup hot tap water
2 teaspoons mild disinfectant
½–1 teaspoon food colour

METHOD
1. Sift dry ingredients into a large microware glass bowl or jug.
2. Add liquids and stir well. Add food dye until desired colour.
3. Microwave on HIGH (90–100%) for 2 minutes, stirring every 30 seconds. Scrape down sides of bowl after stirring. Mixture is ready when it congeals to form a ball.
4. Cover and allow to cool. Store in an airtight container.

POINTER

- Keep, covered, in the fridge to prolong life. Microwave on DEFROST (30–35%) for 1 minute to soften for use.

Sauces

Making sauces in the microwave is virtually foolproof. The indirect heat of the microwave means sauces are much less likely to become lumpy than those cooked conventionally; nor will sauces burn or stick to the bottom of the pan. In addition, there's less washing up after microwaving.

WHITE SAUCE *from 10 months*

A handy basic sauce with a bland flavour and smooth texture, it can be flavoured and used by itself or as the base for other sauces.

INGREDIENTS
2 teaspoons butter
1 teaspoon flour
¼–½ cup milk

METHOD

1. Melt butter in a small microwave-safe jug or bowl on HIGH (90–100%) for 20–30 seconds.
2. Stir in flour thoroughly and cook on HIGH (90–100%) for 30 seconds, stirring twice.
3. Add milk: ¼ cup will make a thick, binding sauce, while ½ cup will make a thinner sauce suitable for pouring. Mix well. Cook on HIGH (90–100%) for 1½ minutes, stirring every 15 seconds.
4. Serve mixed with, or poured over, chicken, fish or vegetables.

VARIATION

- Add finely grated cheese, parsley or 1 small puréed tomato for older children.

POINTER

- Small amounts of butter take a relatively long time to melt in large containers. Melt in small custard cups.

NUTRIENTS
(Average per ½ cup)
Energy 695 kJ (166 kCal)

Nutrient	Amount
Protein	4.60 g
Fat	13.14 g
Carbohydrate	7.99 g
Thiamin	0.07 mg
Riboflavin	0.20 mg
Niacin	0.08 mg
Vitamin C	1.29 mg
Calcium	156.80 mg
Iron	0.18 mg

EASY CHEESE SAUCE

from 10 months

Cheese is part of the 5 food groups recommended for a healthy diet and provides protein, calcium and vitamins. Adding it to sauce makes it easy to mix with other foods and for baby to digest. Makes ¾ cup.

INGREDIENTS

½ cup milk
¼ cup grated cheddar cheese
2 teaspoons cornflour

METHOD

1. Heat milk in a small microwave-safe jug or bowl on HIGH (90–100%) for 1 minute.
2. Toss cheese in flour, add to milk and stir until cheese melts.
3. Microwave on MEDIUM (50–60%) for 1 minute, stirring regularly.

VARIATIONS

- Use mozzarella cheese instead of cheddar.
- Add a small quantity of mild grated parmesan for extra flavour without a lot of fat.

POINTER

- Processed cheese freezes successfully in cooked dishes, but avoid freezing cottage or ricotta cheese.

NUTRIENTS
(Average per ¾ cup)
Energy 1523 kJ (364 kCal)

Nutrient	Amount
Protein	20.77 g
Fat	26.90 g
Carbohydrate	10.54 g
Thiamin	0.08 mg
Riboflavin	0.52 mg
Niacin	0.15 mg
Vitamin C	1.29 mg
Calcium	657.65 mg
Iron	0.36 mg

QUICK TOMATO SAUCE

from 13 months

Home-made is best for baby and is easy to make. Makes 1½ cups.

INGREDIENTS

2 medium-large ripe tomatoes, peeled and chopped
1 level tablespoon ground rice
1 teaspoon finely chopped chives
pinch of basil powder
pinch of oregano powder
¼ cup chicken stock

METHOD

1. Put tomatoes and ground rice in a 4-cup ovenable glass jug.
2. Stir to mix, then add fresh chives and dried herbs.
3. Microwave on HIGH (90–100%) for 3 minutes to blend seasonings, stirring once.
4. Stir in chicken stock. Cover with vented microwave-safe plastic wrap.
5. Cook on HIGH for 4–5 minutes, stirring twice.
6. Sieve, then cool and chill until required.

VARIATIONS

- Use tomato sauce as a dip for finger foods such as vegetables, rusks and bread.
- Add to cooked egg.
- Add to cooked vegetables for extra flavour.

POINTERS

- To skin a tomato easily, heat on HIGH (90–100%) for 45 seconds (until skin splits). Stand for 2–3 minutes, then peel.
- Jugs with handles are the most convenient utensil for cooking sauces in.

NUTRIENTS
(Average per ½ cup)
Energy 211 kJ (50 kCal)

Protein	3.46 g
Fat	0.82 g
Carbohydrate	6.93 g
Thiamin	0.06 mg
Riboflavin	0.05 mg
Niacin	1.35 mg
Vitamin C	24.09 mg
Calcium	12.67 mg
Iron	0.52 mg

POPEYE'S PASTA SAUCE

from 12 months

Spinach is high in iron and the convenience of quality frozen spinach has eliminated the time-consuming careful washing of the leaves. You can offer it as a vegetable, soup or sauce for baby by just using the DEFROST (30–35%) power on your microwave. Makes 4–6 serves.

INGREDIENTS

1 × 250 g packet frozen spinach
1 × 440 g can cream of chicken soup, salt reduced
¼ teaspoon nutmeg
1 cup pine nuts, toasted (optional)

METHOD

1. Thaw spinach in its packet on DEFROST (30–35%) for 5 minutes.
2. Mix soup, spinach and nutmeg together in a medium microware container. Microwave on HIGH (90–100%) for 5–6 minutes, stirring occasionally.
3. Purée mixture. Toss in pine nuts and serve over cooked wholemeal or plain spiral noodles.

VARIATION

- Spinach can be mixed into White Sauce (p. 145).

POINTER

- Toast pine nuts by scattering ½ cup onto an ovenable glass pie plate and heating on HIGH (90–100%) for 2–4 minutes, stirring several times to prevent burning.

NUTRIENTS
(Average per serve)
Energy 767 kJ (183 kCal)

Protein	11.90 g
Fat	40.31 g
Carbohydrate	9.9 g
Thiamin	0.34 mg
Riboflavin	0.30 mg
Niacin	2.84 mg
Vitamin C	10.00 mg
Calcium	78.55 mg
Iron	3.14 mg

PUMPKIN PASTA SAUCE

from 19 months

A colourful sauce for plain or wholemeal cooked pasta. Makes about 1½ cups.

INGREDIENTS
100 g skinless chicken
100 g pumpkin
¾ cup chicken stock
2 teaspoons cornflour
1 tablespoon toasted sesame seeds

METHOD

1. Chop chicken and pumpkin into 2-cm pieces. Place in a medium microwave container. Pour over ½ cup stock.
2. Cover with lid. Microwave on HIGH (90–100%) for 2 minutes. Stir. Reduce power to MEDIUM (50–60%) and cook for 5 minutes.
3. Purée pumpkin and chicken mixture.
4. Blend cornflour in remaining stock until dissolved. Microwave on HIGH (90–100%) for 1½ minutes, stirring regularly until thickened.
5. Add pumpkin mixture, stir well. Microwave on HIGH (90–100%) for 1 minute.
6. Serve over pasta of your choice and sprinkle with toasted sesame seeds.

FREEZING

- Freeze in ½-cup quantities.
- DEFROST (30-35%) for 5 minutes per ½ cup.

POINTER

- Toast sesame seeds in the microwave oven by scattering over an ovenable glass pie dish and microwaving on HIGH (90-100%) in 30-second bursts and stirring to prevent burning. 2 tablespoons sesame seeds will take about 1 minute.

NUTRIENTS
(Average per ½ cup)
Energy 440 kJ (105 kCal)

Nutrient	Amount
Protein	11.29 g
Fat	4.31 g
Carbohydrate	5.67 g
Thiamin	0.10 mg
Riboflavin	0.09 mg
Niacin	3.40 mg
Vitamin C	2.66 mg
Calcium	72.17 mg
Iron	0.91 mg

REAL TOMATO SAUCE

from 13 months

This takes a little longer than Quick Tomato Sauce (p. 147), but is delicious. Makes about 2 cups.

INGREDIENTS
1 onion, grated
1 tablespoon oil
1 stick celery, finely chopped
500 g ripe tomatoes, peeled and chopped
1–3 tablespoons tomato paste
½ teaspoon ground thyme
1 tablespoon finely chopped parsley
1 teaspoon dark brown sugar

METHOD
1. Combine onion and oil in 4-cup ovenable glass jug and microwave on HIGH (90–100%) for 2½ minutes.
2. Stir in the celery and microwave on HIGH (90–100%) for 2½ minutes.
3. Add tomatoes, tomato paste (the more you add the richer the colour will become), herbs and sugar. Cover and microwave on HIGH (90–100%) for 5 minutes.
4. Stir, re-cover and microwave on HIGH (90–100%) for a further 5 minutes.
5. Cool and blend well until smooth. Store in the refrigerator in a sterilised screw-top jar.

VARIATION
- For older children and adults, garlic, basil and oregano can be added with the other herbs to give a lively flavour.

POINTER
- Commercial tomato sauce in bottles can be warmed to a pouring consistency by removing metal lid and heating the bottle in the microwave on HIGH (90-100%) for 30-60 seconds.

NUTRIENTS
(Average per ½ cup)
Energy 311 kJ (74 kCal)

Nutrient	Amount
Protein	2.08 g
Fat	4.92 g
Carbohydrate	5.38 g
Thiamin	0.08 mg
Riboflavin	0.04 mg
Niacin	1.19 mg
Vitamin C	30.06 mg
Calcium	24.36 mg
Iron	0.80 mg

KIWI FRUIT SAUCE

from 9 months

This fruit is available all year round and is a colourful source of Vitamin C and potassium.

INGREDIENTS

5 kiwi fruit

1 pear, peeled, cored and stewed (p. 54)

METHOD

1. Peel and thinly slice kiwi fruit. Place in a medium-size microware container.
2. Cover and microwave on HIGH (90–100%) for 6 minutes, stirring twice.
3. Cool and blend together with stewed pear until smooth.

VARIATIONS

- Add 1 teaspoon apple concentrate to sweeten for babies.
- For twelve months and over, add 1 teaspoon honey to sweeten. Serve with yoghurt.

POINTER

- Kiwi fruit can be served raw, peeled and sliced.

NUTRIENTS

(Average per ½ cup)

Energy 305 kJ (73 kCal)

Nutrient	Amount
Protein	1.82 g
Fat	0.26 g
Carbohydrate	15.66 g
Thiamin	0.02 mg
Riboflavin	0.06 mg
Niacin	0.53 mg
Vitamin C	93.95 mg
Calcium	31.20 mg
Iron	0.67 mg

CUSTARD SAUCE *from 12 months*

A convenient sauce that is always popular.

INGREDIENTS

2 teaspoons custard powder
½ cup milk
1 teaspoon sugar

METHOD

1. Blend custard powder with a little milk to dissolve.
2. Heat remaining milk in a small microwave-safe jug on HIGH (90–100%) for 1 minute.
3. Add custard and sugar, stir well. Cook on HIGH (90–100%) for 1½ minutes, stirring regularly.
4. Serve over puddings or stewed fruit.

VARIATIONS

- **Banana custard** Use 3 teaspoons custard powder and stir through ½ banana, sliced, when custard is cooked.
- **Chocolate custard** Add 1 teaspoon cocoa to the custard powder and use 2 teaspoons sugar.
- **Egg custard** Add 1 × 55 g egg at the end of cooking time. Whisk well to prevent scrambling.

POINTER

- The lack of direct heat in a microwave reduces the amount of stirring required to make a lump-free custard quickly.

NUTRIENTS
(Average per ½ cup)
Energy 486 kJ (116 kCal)

Nutrient	Amount
Protein	4.26 g
Fat	4.93 g
Carbohydrate	13.97 g
Thiamin	0.07 mg
Riboflavin	0.19 mg
Niacin	0.02 mg
Vitamin C	1.29 mg
Calcium	155.27 mg
Iron	0.17 mg

ALL SEASONS FRUIT SAUCE (F)

from 2 years

Make this ahead and store in the refrigerator until ready to use. Makes 1⅔ cups.

INGREDIENTS

1/2 cup dried pawpaw
1 1/4 cups unsweetened pineapple juice
1/3 cup castor sugar
1–2 tablespoons lemon juice
1/4 teaspoon cinnamon

METHOD

1. In a 4-cup ovenable glass jug, combine pawpaw, pineapple juice, sugar and lemon juice.
2. Cover with vented plastic wrap. Microwave on HIGH (90–100%) for 6 minutes, stirring twice.
3. Let stand for 5 minutes, then blend until smooth and thickened.

VARIATION

- Sauce can be made with dried apricots, apples or pears.

POINTER

- To soften dried fruit, place 1 cup fruit with ¼ cup water in a 2-cup ovenable glass jug. Microwave, covered, on HIGH (90–100%) for 1 minute, then stand for 1 minute before using.

NUTRIENTS
(Average per ½ cup)
Energy 603 kJ (144 kCal)

Nutrient	Amount
Protein	0.62 g
Fat	0.15 g
Carbohydrate	35.16 g
Thiamin	0.06 mg
Riboflavin	0.04 mg
Niacin	0.36 mg
Vitamin C	47.33 mg
Calcium	20.93 mg
Iron	0.56 mg

RHUBARB SAUCE *from 13 months*

Rhubarb is a good source of vitamins A and C, as well as potassium and magnesium. Try this sauce over some home-made ice cream. Makes ¾ cup.

INGREDIENTS
100 g rhubarb
juice of 1 orange
1 teaspoon honey

METHOD

1. Remove leaves and base of rhubarb stalk. Cut into 2-cm pieces. Place in a small microware container with orange juice and honey. Cover with lid.
2. Cook on HIGH (90–100%) for 4 minutes, stirring occasionally.
3. Purée sauce and dilute with a little water, if necessary. Serve over ice cream or mixed with yoghurt.
4. Store excess in refrigerator.

VARIATION

- Serve over poached fruit or mix with yoghurt.

POINTER

- Soften ice cream by placing a 1-litre carton on the turntable and heating on LOW (30–40%) for 30–40 seconds until soft enough for serving.

NUTRIENTS
(Average per ¾ cup)
Energy 345 kJ (82 kCal)

Protein	2.42 g
Fat	0.45 g
Carbohydrate	16.29 g
Thiamin	0.19 mg
Riboflavin	0.08 mg
Niacin	0.97 mg
Vitamin C	87.05 mg
Calcium	36.54 mg
Iron	0.71 mg

Cakes, biscuits and muffins

Microwave cakes are easy and quick to make – taking just a few minutes. They are moist and tender if not overcooked. Here are a few tips to help you achieve the best results if you have never baked cakes before in your microwave oven.

- Cakes do not brown or develop a crust during microwave cooking, so top with a sauce, fruit, browned coconut or finely ground nuts for an attractive finish.
- Line cake dishes with white paper towel rather than greasing and sugaring. Fat and sugar both heat quickly, diverting microwaves away from the cake batter.
- Fill cake containers no more than half full, as microwave cakes expand more than conventionally cooked ones.
- Cakes cook best in round dishes rather than square ones. A special microwave cake-ring ensures cakes cook in the time given in recipes.
- Allow cake batters to rest for 5–10 minutes after preparation. This helps the top of the cake cook more evenly.
- Cakes cook best if elevated so microwaves can penetrate from underneath the container. They also need moving several times during cooking to ensure even results. If you open the oven door during cooking the cake will not fall as microwave ovens cook by power and not heat.
- Leave cakes in the oven after baking, or cool on a flat surface, to help cook the bottom right through.
- Refrigerate baked cakes to keep fresh.
- Cakes can be frozen whole in microwave-safe bags, or as individual slices in plastic wrap.

APPLE CAKE *from 18 months*

Make this cake anytime because it's so quick. Sauce it for added flair and flavour. Makes 8 slices.

INGREDIENTS

1 butter cake packet mix
2 eggs
2 medium Granny Smith apples
2 teaspoons cinnamon

METHOD

1. Make up packet mix as directed, adding an extra egg for moisture.
2. Peel and slice the apples. Place half the slices around the base of a 20-cm microware ring container, dust with 1 teaspoon cinnamon and microwave on HIGH (90–100%) for 1 minute to soften.
3. Pour half the batter over the blanched apples and spread the rest of the raw apples over this mix. Sprinkle with cinnamon and top with balance of batter.
4. Cover, elevate container on roasting rack (or upturned saucer) and place off the centre of the turntable. Microwave on HIGH (90–100%) for 5 minutes, moving dish to opposite side of the turntable halfway through cooking.
5. Stand until cake is cold. Invert onto serving platter and dust with cinnamon.

VARIATION

- Top with orange or lemon sauce. Mix ½ cup castor sugar and 1 tablespoon cornflour with 1 cup water in a 4-cup jug. Heat on HIGH (90–100%) for 2–2½ minutes, stirring regularly. Blend in 2 tablespoons butter, 1½ tablespoons orange or lemon juice and ½ teaspoon grated orange or lemon rind.

FREEZING

- Store one whole cake in microwave-safe freezer bag.
- DEFROST (30-35%) whole cake for 2 minutes, in 10-second bursts. Stand for half an hour.
- For one slice of cake (100 g) wrapped in microwave-safe plastic wrap, DEFROST (30–35%) for 1–1½ minutes. Turn over once. Stand for 10 minutes.

POINTERS

- Cakes do not form a crust when baked in a microwave oven, but when covered with fruit, sauce or icing no-one knows.
- Store by wrapping in plastic wrap and keeping in the refrigerator.

NUTRIENTS
(Average per slice)
Energy 745 kJ (178 kCal)

Nutrient	Amount
Protein	4.17 g
Fat	4.49 g
Carbohydrate	30.69 g
Thiamin	0.05 mg
Riboflavin	0.10 mg
Niacin	0.27 mg
Vitamin C	1.95 mg
Calcium	26.32 mg
Iron	0.79 mg

THE CARROT CAKE

from 2 years

A real winner, and a great way of co-opting non-carrot-eating children and adults into getting some Vitamin A. Makes 8–10 slices.

INGREDIENTS

1 cup brown sugar
1 cup light olive oil
1 teaspoon vanilla essence
3 eggs
1½ cups self-raising flour
1 teaspoon baking powder
1½ teaspoons cinnamon
2 cups shredded carrots
½ cup walnuts, chopped or ground (optional)
250 g unsweetened pineapple, crushed and drained
¼ cup ground walnuts, for dusting

METHOD

1. In a large bowl, mix together sugar, oil, vanilla and eggs. Sift in flour, baking powder and cinnamon, blending well. Add carrots, walnuts and pineapple, combining until mixed. Let batter rest for 10 minutes.
2. Line the base of a 20-cm microware cake-ring with paper towel and pour in batter. Cover, elevate on roasting rack (or upturned saucer) and place off the centre of the turntable.
3. Microwave on MEDIUM-HIGH (70–80%) for 12 minutes, moving the container to the opposite side of the turntable halfway through cooking.
4. Stand until cold. Invert onto a serving platter and remove paper towel from the base. Dust with ground walnuts.

FREEZING

- Store whole cake in microwave-safe freezer bag.
- DEFROST (30-35%) whole cake for 2 minutes in 10-second bursts. Stand for half an hour.
- For one slice of cake (100 g) wrapped in micro-wave-safe plastic wrap, DEFROST (30–35%) for 1–1½ minutes. Turn over once. Stand for 10 minutes.

POINTER

- Cakes cook best in round dishes.

NUTRIENTS
(Average per slice)
Energy 1953 kJ (466 kCal)

Nutrient	Amount
Protein	5.97 g
Fat	33.46 g
Carbohydrate	36.29 g
Thiamin	0.13 mg
Riboflavin	0.10 mg
Niacin	0.60 mg
Vitamin C	6.71 mg
Calcium	52.17 mg
Iron	0.94 mg

'OKAY FOR KIDS' CHOCOLATE CAKE

from 2 years

This easy home-made cake is ideal for a second birthday. Makes 8 slices.

INGREDIENTS

1 cup self-raising flour
3/4 cup castor sugar
1 tablespoon carob powder
1/4 cup butter, melted
2/3 cup milk
1 teaspoon vanilla essence
2 eggs, beaten
toasted coconut

METHOD

1. Place all the dry ingredients in a mixing bowl.
2. Stir in melted butter, milk, eggs and vanilla.
3. Mix well with a fork until batter is smooth. Line the base of a 20-cm microware cake-ring with paper towel and pour the batter into the pan.
4. Cover, elevate on a roasting rack (or upturned saucer) and microwave off the centre of the turntable on HIGH (90–100%) for 4½ minutes.
5. Move to the opposite side of the turntable and microwave on MEDIUM (50–60%) for 4 minutes.
6. Stand until cold and invert onto a serving plate. Decorate with toasted coconut.

VARIATION

- Use cocoa in place of carob powder.

FREEZING

- DEFROST (30–35%) whole cake for 2 minutes in 10-second bursts. Stand for half an hour.
- For one slice of cake (100 g) wrapped in micro-wave-save plastic wrap, DEFROST (30–35%) for 1–1½ minutes. Turn over once. Stand for 10 minutes.

POINTER

- Coconut can be toasted in the microwave by scattering 1 cup on a microware-safe plate and cooking on HIGH (90–100%) for 2–3 minutes. Stir frequently to prevent burning.

NUTRIENTS
(Average per slice)
Energy 967 kJ (231 kCal)

Nutrient	Amount
Protein	3.45 g
Fat	9.38 g
Carbohydrate	33.25 g
Thiamin	0.05 mg
Riboflavin	0.06 mg
Niacin	0.24 mg
Vitamin C	0.00 mg
Calcium	32.46 mg
Iron	0.54 mg

GOLDEN GINGERBREAD CAKE

from 2 years

Golden Delicious apples are a favourite for baking in cakes, and for cooking in general, because they hold their shape. Makes 8 slices.

INGREDIENTS

1 packet gingerbread cake mix
2 eggs
1 cup finely chopped Golden Delicious apple
½ cup walnuts, finely ground or chopped (optional)
1 tablespoon walnuts, extra finely ground for dusting

METHOD

1. Make up packet mix as directed, adding an extra egg for moisture.
2. Stir in chopped apple and walnuts. Mix with a fork for 1 minute so ingredients are blended well. Batter should be a uniform colour and consistency.
3. Line a 20-cm round cake-ring dish with paper towel and pour batter into prepared pan. Cover.
4. Elevate container on a roasting rack (or upturned saucer). Place off the centre of the turntable.
5. Microwave on HIGH (90–100%) for 5 minutes, moving dish to opposite side of the turntable halfway through the cooking time.
6. Stand cake until cold. Invert onto a serving platter. Remove paper from base. Dust with ground nuts.

VARIATION

- Use a finely chopped firm pear in place of the apple.

FREEZING

- Store one whole cake in microwave-safe freezer bag.
- DEFROST (30-35%) cake for 2 minutes in 10-second bursts. Stand for half an hour.
- For one slice of cake (100 g) wrapped in microwave-safe plastic wrap, DEFROST (30–35%) for 1–1½ minutes. Turn over once. Stand for 10 minutes.

NUTRIENTS
(Average per slice)
Energy 1068 kJ (255 kCal)

Nutrient	Amount
Protein	5.80 g
Fat	12.54 g
Carbohydrate	30.54 g
Thiamin	0.09 mg
Riboflavin	0.12 mg
Niacin	0.42 mg
Vitamin C	1.54 mg
Calcium	34.82 mg
Iron	1.14 mg

ZUCCHINI CAKE *from 2 years*

This cake is a change from the more traditional carrot cake and can be enjoyed by the whole family. Makes 10 slices.

INGREDIENTS

3 eggs
1½ cups castor sugar
1 cup light olive oil
1 teaspoon vanilla essence
1½ cups self-raising flour
1 teaspoon baking powder
2 teaspoons cinnamon
2 cups grated zucchini
½ cup walnuts, chopped or ground
¼ cup ground walnuts for dusting

METHOD

1. In a large bowl combine eggs, sugar, oil and vanilla. Sift in flour, baking powder and cinnamon. Fold in zucchini and nuts.
2. Line the base of a 20-cm microware cake-ring with white paper towel. Pour batter into prepared pan.
3. Cover, elevate on a roasting rack (or upturned saucer) and place off the centre of the turntable. Microwave on MEDIUM-HIGH (70–80%) for 12 minutes, moving the container to the opposite side of the turntable halfway through cooking.
4. Stand until cold. Invert onto a serving platter and remove paper towel from base. Dust with ground walnuts.

FREEZING

- Store whole cake in microwave-safe freezer bag.
- DEFROST (30-35%) for 2 minutes in 10-second bursts. Stand for half an hour.
- For one slice of cake (100 g) wrapped in microwave-safe plastic wrap, DEFROST (30–35%) for 1–1½ minutes. Turn over once. Stand for 10 minutes.

NUTRIENTS
(Average per slice)
Energy 2151 kJ (514 kCal)

Nutrient	Amount
Protein	5.89 g
Fat	34.50 g
Carbohydrate	45.95 g
Thiamin	0.11 mg
Riboflavin	0.10 mg
Niacin	0.53 mg
Vitamin C	4.03 mg
Calcium	42.55 mg
Iron	0.94 mg

OATMEAL SLICE *from 2 years*

Quick-cooking breakfast oats form the base of this handy home-made slice. Makes 8 slices.

INGREDIENTS
1¼ cups water
1 cup quick-cooking oats
½ cup butter, melted
1 cup dark brown sugar
2 eggs, beaten
1 teaspoon vanilla essence
1¼ cups self-raising flour
1 teaspoon baking powder
1 teaspoon cinnamon
½ cup toasted coconut

METHOD

1. In a 4-cup jug, heat water on HIGH (90–100%) for 2½–3 minutes to boil. Stir in oats and stand for 15 minutes.
2. Mix together butter and sugar until fluffy. Stir into oat mixture. Add remaining ingredients except coconut and mix well.
3. Line the base of a large microware container with white paper towel and pour the batter into the pan. Cover, elevate container on a roasting rack (or upturned saucer) and place in the centre of the turntable.
4. Microwave on HIGH (90–100%) for 10–11 minutes until the centre is cooked through.
5. Stand until cold. Invert onto a serving platter and remove paper towel from the base. Dust with toasted coconut.

VARIATION

- ½ cup ground or finely chopped nuts can be added to this mix, or used for dusting for children over two years.

FREEZING

- DEFROST (30–35%) whole cake for 2 minutes in 10-second bursts. Stand for half an hour.
- For one slice (100 g) wrapped in microwave-safe plastic wrap, DEFROST (30-35%) for 1-1½ minutes. Turn over once. Stand for 10 minutes.

POINTERS

- Coconut can be toasted in the microwave by scattering 1 cup on a microware-safe plate and cooking on HIGH (90–100%) for 2–3 minutes. Stir frequently to prevent burning.
- Use coconut for older children only and take care they do not inhale it.

NUTRIENTS
(Average per slice)
Energy 1525 kJ (364 kCal)

Nutrient	Amount
Protein	5.27 g
Fat	18.28 g
Carbohydrate	44.96 g
Thiamin	0.12 mg
Riboflavin	0.07 mg
Niacin	0.41 mg
Vitamin C	0.00 mg
Calcium	37.27 mg
Iron	1.03 mg

APRICOT CRACKLE SLICE

from 2 years

Apricots are a source of Vitamin A and mix well with other ingredients, especially when puréed.

INGREDIENTS
60 g butter
10 Granita biscuits, crushed
200 g dried apricots
1¼ cups water
1 teaspoon gelatine
1 teaspoon honey
30 g copha
2 tablespoons honey
1½ cups Rice Bubbles
½ cup desiccated coconut

METHOD

1. Melt butter in a medium microware container on HIGH (90–100%) for 30–40 seconds.
2. Add biscuit crumbs and mix thoroughly. Press firmly over base of 18 × 28 cm ovenable glass dish.
3. Place apricots and water in a medium microware container. Microwave on HIGH (90–100%) for 2 minutes, then MEDIUM (50–60%) for 5–6 minutes. Water will almost have been absorbed and apricots will be plump and soft.
4. Add gelatine to apricots. Mix well with a fork or purée. Spread over biscuit base.
5. Melt copha in a medium container on MEDIUM-HIGH (70–80%) for 2 minutes or until melted. Add honey, mix well. Add Rice Bubbles and coconut, stir thoroughly. Spoon over apricots, smooth surface.
6. Chill to set. Cut into about 15 fingers or squares.

VARIATION

- Use plums in place of apricots when in season and add an extra teaspoon of gelatine to the purée.

POINTER

- Chopping copha into pieces helps it to melt quickly in the microwave oven.

NUTRIENTS
(Average per slice)
Energy 564 kJ (135 kCal)

Nutrient	Amount
Protein	1.33 g
Fat	11.13 g
Carbohydrate	15.49 g
Thiamin	0.04 mg
Riboflavin	0.06 mg
Niacin	0.78 mg
Vitamin C	0.00 mg
Calcium	15.57 mg
Iron	0.97 mg

PEANUT BUTTER COOKIES *from 2 years*

These cookies don't require baking but set in the freezer in a couple of hours. Makes 36 cookies.

INGREDIENTS

½ cup melted butter
½ cup milk
1 cup castor sugar
½ cup smooth peanut butter
1 teaspoon vanilla essence
3 cups instant oats
1 cup finely ground peanuts

METHOD

1. In a large microwave-safe bowl, combine butter and milk and microwave on HIGH (90–100%) for 45 seconds.
2. Blend in sugar and microwave on MEDIUM (50–60%) for 2 minutes to dissolve.
3. Add peanut butter and vanilla, stirring to mix together well. Blend in oats.
4. Drop 1 teaspoon at a time onto a foil sheet and refrigerate 1–2 hours until firm.
5. When firm, dust with ground nuts. Store in the refrigerator.

VARIATION

- For parties, press a jelly bean or Smartie into the top of each cookie.

POINTER

- Soften peanut butter for easy mixing by removing lid from the jar and heating on HIGH (90–100%) for 1 minute per 250 g.

NUTRIENTS
(Average per cookie)
Energy 445 kJ (106 kCal)

Nutrient	Amount
Protein	1.97 g
Fat	6.02 g
Carbohydrate	11.21 g
Thiamin	0.05 mg
Riboflavin	0.02 mg
Niacin	0.73 mg
Vitamin C	0.04 mg
Calcium	10.15 mg
Iron	0.40 mg

DATE 'N' ORANGE BRAN BREAD *from 2 years*

Dates contain over 60 per cent natural sugars and are high in fibre. Use the semi-dried boxed dates for this healthy brown bread. Makes 8 slices.

INGREDIENTS

¾ cup dates, finely chopped
1 cup oat bran
2 tablespoons melted butter
¼ cup honey
¾ cup hot water
1 egg
1 cup self-raising flour
1 teaspoon baking powder
2 teaspoons grated orange rind

METHOD

1. In a large bowl, place dates, bran, butter, honey, hot water and the egg. Beat well. Add flour, baking powder and orange rind. Mix until combined.
2. Line the base of a 20-cm microware cake-ring dish with paper towel, spoon in batter and cover. Elevate container on a roasting rack (or upturned saucer) and place off the centre of the turntable.
3. Microwave on HIGH (90–100%) for 6 minutes, moving dish to the opposite side of the turntable halfway through cooking.
4. Stand until cold. Invert bread onto a serving dish and remove paper towel. Slice and serve.

VARIATION

- Use orange juice in place of water.

POINTER

- Being high in sugar, dates are attractive to microwaves. Make sure they are well distributed through the batter to prevent burnt spots.

NUTRIENTS
(Average per serve)
Energy 847 kJ (202 kCal)

Nutrient	Amount
Protein	5.72 g
Fat	6.12 g
Carbohydrate	38.19 g
Thiamin	0.25 mg
Riboflavin	0.08 mg
Niacin	0.59 mg
Vitamin C	1.25 mg
Calcium	39.22 mg
Iron	1.40 mg

BANANA MUFFINS *from 2 years*

These aromatic muffins melt in the mouth, especially when warm. Makes approximately 15 muffins.

INGREDIENTS
90 g butter
1/3 cup brown sugar
1 1/2 cups wholemeal self-raising flour
2 eggs, lightly beaten
2 ripe bananas, mashed
cinnamon sugar

METHOD
1. Melt butter in a large jug or bowl on HIGH (90–100%) for 1 minute.
2. Add sugar, mix well to dissolve any lumps. Add flour, eggs and banana. Mix with a fork to combine. Do not over beat.
3. Two-thirds fill each cavity of a muffin pan. Elevate on a roasting rack (or upturned saucer). Microwave on HIGH (90–100%) for 1½ minutes for 5 muffins.
4. Stand for 2 minutes before removing from pan. Sprinkle with a little cinnamon sugar.
5. Repeat procedure twice with remaining mixture.

FREEZING
- Wrap muffins individually in microwave-safe plastic wrap.
- DEFROST (30-35%) for 15 seconds each.

POINTERS
- Line cavity of muffin tray with a white paper patty case to absorb excess moisture, to give a traditional muffin shape and to aid freezing.
- Ripe bananas mash well in their skins by kneading well with fingers before peeling and scooping out flesh.

NUTRIENTS
(Average per muffin)
Energy 555 kJ (133 kCal)

Nutrient	Amount
Protein	2.95 g
Fat	5.86 g
Carbohydrate	16.82 g
Thiamin	0.08 mg
Riboflavin	0.06 mg
Niacin	0.90 mg
Vitamin C	2.21 mg
Calcium	8.96 mg
Iron	0.65 mg

BRAN MUFFINS *from 2 years*

Just the right size for small hands. Cover cooked muffins with microwave-safe plastic wrap to keep them fresh. Makes 6 muffins.

INGREDIENTS
1 cup wheatbran cereal
½ cup milk
½ cup self-raising flour
1 teaspoon baking powder
1 cup firmly packed brown sugar
2 eggs, beaten
3 tablespoons light olive oil

METHOD
1. Line six custard cups with paper liners.
2. Combine cereal and milk and let stand for 5 minutes.
3. In a large bowl mix flour, baking powder and brown sugar.
4. Combine the eggs and oil. Add to cereal mixture and stir until well mixed. Add cereal mixture to flour mixture and blend thoroughly.
5. Spoon a generous tablespoon into each custard cup. Place cups in a circle on the rim of the turntable.
6. Microwave on MEDIUM-HIGH (70–80%) for 3 minutes, rotating cups halfway through cooking time.
7. Let stand until completely cold before removing muffins in paper from cups.

VARIATION
- Use oat bran in place of wheat bran.

POINTER
- To warm one muffin in the microwave, wrap in microwave-safe plastic wrap and heat on MEDIUM (50–60%) for 20 seconds.

NUTRIENTS
(Average per muffin)
Energy 1222 kJ (292 kCal)

Nutrient	Amount
Protein	5.60 g
Fat	12.48 g
Carbohydrate	39.53 g
Thiamin	0.11 mg
Riboflavin	0.13 mg
Niacin	2.55 mg
Vitamin C	0.21 mg
Calcium	53.95 mg
Iron	1.62 mg

Snacks

The microwave oven is ideal for making speedy snacks or wholesome fast food, for healthy young appetites. Have fun watching some fat-free corn 'pop', or satisfy a sweet tooth with a little ice cream cone cake, which takes just 30 seconds to cook!

STRAWBERRY JELLY

from 8 months

Babies love jelly. Keep some on hand in the refrigerator for special snacks. Makes ½ cup.

INGREDIENTS

1 punnet strawberries (about 300 g)
juice of ½ lemon (optional)
1 teaspoon gelatine

METHOD

1. Wash and hull strawberries. Place in a 4-cup microwave-safe jug, together with lemon juice if using.
2. Place jug off the centre of the turntable and microwave on MEDIUM-HIGH (70–80%) for 5 minutes.
3. Stir and microwave on HIGH (90–100%) for 5 minutes.
4. Place a fine sieve over a clean glass jug and pour cooked strawberries into it. Allow juice to drip through into the jug (about 10 minutes).
5. Stir gelatine into warm berry juice and microwave on HIGH (90–100%) for 30 seconds.
6. Stir well to dissolve and distribute gelatine, then pour into sterilised jar. Store in refrigerator.

VARIATION

- This jelly can be made with the berries of your choice.

POINTERS

- Spread on a rusk, toast or bread.
- Sterilise a small jar to store the jelly in the microwave. Half fill with water and heat for 2–3 minutes on HIGH (90–100%). Remove from oven with mitts, empty and turn upside down to drain on paper towel.

NUTRIENTS
(Average per teaspoon)
Energy 13 kJ (3 kCal)

Nutrient	Amount
Protein	0.26 g
Fat	0.01 g
Carbohydrate	0.44 g
Thiamin	0.00 mg
Riboflavin	0.01 mg
Niacin	0.62 mg
Vitamin C	7.75 mg
Calcium	2.11 mg
Iron	0.09 mg

POPCORN *from 18 months*

This is fun to watch cook as well as being a fat-free way of making a popular snack.

INGREDIENTS
¼ cup popping corn
1 teaspoon water

METHOD
1. Place corn and water in a 4-litre ovenable jug. Cover with microwave container lid.
2. Place off the centre of the turntable. Microwave on HIGH (90–100%) for 5–5½ minutes. Remove when 'popping' has finished – be careful, as the jug will be hot.

VARIATION
- Toss through hundreds and thousands.

POINTER
- Popcorn will cook more quickly in a plastic 2.5-litre microware container. Microwave on HIGH (90–100%) for approximately 4–4½ minutes.

NUTRIENTS
(Average per serve)
Energy 97 kJ (23 kCal)

Protein	1.05 g
Fat	0.30 g
Carbohydrate	3.97 g
Thiamin	0.05 mg
Riboflavin	0.02 mg
Niacin	0.13 mg
Vitamin C	1.50 mg
Calcium	5.50 mg
Iron	0.52 mg

CHICKEN NIBBLES

from 15 months

Chicken ribs or drumlets are just the right size for junior, as well as being safe and easy to chew on.

INGREDIENTS

1 tablespoon lemon juice
2 teaspoons honey
1 teaspoon light soy sauce
250 g chicken drumlets, ribs or satay pieces

METHOD

1. Blend marinade ingredients together thoroughly.
2. Remove skin from chicken, marinate in a small microware dish for several hours or overnight, turning occasionally.
3. Microwave on HIGH (90–100%) for 1 minute. Rotate chicken pieces and brush with sauce.
4. Microwave on HIGH (90–100%) for a further 1 minute. Stand for 2 minutes.
5. Remove chicken to a serving plate. Strain marinade through a fine sieve. Microwave on HIGH (90–100%) for 3 minutes, stirring occasionally, to reduce to a thick sauce. Brush over chicken. Serve warm or cold.

VARIATIONS

- Instead of reducing marinade, thicken with a little cornflour and serve as a dipping sauce.
- Small chicken drumsticks may be used. Allow 1¾–2 minutes per leg on HIGH (90–100%).
- An alternative sweet 'n' sour marinade can be made by combining 1 tablespoon tomato sauce, 1 tablespoon pineapple juice, 1 teaspoon vinegar and, optionally, a pinch of Chinese five-spice powder.

POINTERS

- Cooking time may vary depending on thickness of chicken. Adequate standing time will ensure chicken cooks right through.
- If using drumsticks for toddlers, watch for the sharp needle-like bone running parallel to the main bone. It should be removed for safety.

NUTRIENTS
(Average per 100 g)
Energy 810 kJ (193 kCal)

Nutrient	Amount
Protein	24.56 g
Fat	9.15 g
Carbohydrate	3.35 g
Thiamin	0.07 mg
Riboflavin	0.26 mg
Niacin	4.22 mg
Vitamin C	2.57 mg
Calcium	18.69 mg
Iron	1.15 mg

MINI DIM SIMS *from 21 months*

Steamed dim sims are done simply in the microwave as no water is required.

INGREDIENTS

3 frozen mini dim sims

METHOD

1. Run water over each dim sim and drain away excess water.
2. Place dim sims on a small plate or dish.
3. Cover tightly with plastic wrap.
4. Microwave on MEDIUM (50–60%) for 3 minutes. Stand 1 minute. Serve as a snack.

VARIATIONS

- Dip mini dim sims into fresh tomato sauce.
- Add dim sims to chicken stock for a delicious soup on a cold day.

POINTER

- For fast food for adults, dim sims can be steamed on HIGH (90–100%) for 30 seconds each and dipped into soy sauce.

NUTRIENTS

(Average per dim sim)

Energy 309 kJ (74 kCal)

Protein	3.40 g
Fat	2.53 g
Carbohydrate	8.67 g
Thiamin	0.03 mg
Riboflavin	0.02 mg
Niacin	0.50 mg
Vitamin C	1.00 mg
Calcium	22.33 mg
Iron	0.70 mg

SWEETCORN ON THE COB (F)

from 2 years

Young ears of corn picked before the grain is fully ripe cook beautifully in the microwave, retaining a vibrant golden yellow colour whilst providing a nutritionally healthy meal.

INGREDIENTS

1 small cob of corn, with leaves intact
1 tablespoon melted butter

METHOD

1. Fold back the leaves, remove the silk tassels and rinse.
2. Re-cover with the leaves and place on the edge of the turntable.
3. Microwave on HIGH (90–100%) for 3 minutes, turning over halfway through cooking time.
4. Stand for 1–2 minutes, remove leaves and brush with melted butter.

VARIATION

- Adults may like to season melted butter with freshly crushed garlic or finely chopped herbs.

POINTER

- The sweetcorn kernels can be stripped from the cob and cooked on HIGH (90–100%) for 4–6 minutes per 250 g.

NUTRIENTS
(Average per cob)
Energy 1078 kJ (258 kCal)

Protein	2.46 g
Fat	18.01 g
Carbohydrate	21.93 g
Thiamin	0.09 mg
Riboflavin	0.06 mg
Niacin	1.62 mg
Vitamin C	3.40 mg
Calcium	5.55 mg
Iron	0.46 mg

LITTLE ICE CREAM CONE CAKES

from 18 months

A packet cake is a handy back-up as a snack. Prepared batter will keep for one month in the refrigerator if tightly covered.

INGREDIENTS

1 flat-bottomed ice-cream cone
2 tablespoons cake batter
hundreds and thousands for decorating

METHOD

1. Two-thirds fill ice-cream cone with cake batter.
2. Place cone off the centre of the turntable and microwave on HIGH (90–100%) for 20–30 seconds. Cake should rise above sides of cone.
3. Stand for 30 seconds, then sprinkle with hundreds and thousands.

VARIATION

- Microwave 2 cones for 45 seconds on HIGH (90–100%); 3 cones for 1 minute on HIGH (90–100%); 4 cones for 1¼ minutes on HIGH (90–100%).

POINTER

- An extra egg improves the finish of a microwave-baked packet cake.

NUTRIENTS
(Average per cone)
Energy 283 kJ (68 kCal)

Nutrient	Amount
Protein	1.30 g
Fat	1.24 g
Carbohydrate	12.91 g
Thiamin	0.01 mg
Riboflavin	0.02 mg
Niacin	0.19 mg
Vitamin C	0.00 mg
Calcium	8.02 mg
Iron	0.29 mg

ANY BERRY JAM *from 18 months*

Cook small quantities at a time and store in the refrigerator. Makes 1 cup.

INGREDIENTS

1 punnet strawberries (about 300 g) or berry of choice
juice of 1 lemon
1 cup castor sugar
1 tablespoon pectin

METHOD

1. Hull strawberries and rinse.
2. Place together with lemon juice in a 6-cup microwave-safe jug and cook on HIGH (90–100%) for 5 minutes.
3. Stir in sugar and microwave on HIGH (90–100%) for 5 minutes.
4. Stir in pectin and microwave on HIGH (90–100%) for 5 minutes, stirring once.
5. Cool and pot in sterilised jar.

VARIATION

- Use blackberries, raspberries or loganberries instead of strawberries.

POINTER

- Sterilise a jar to store the jam in the microwave. Half fill with water and heat for 2-3 minutes on HIGH (90-100%) to boil water. Remove from oven with mitts, empty and turn upside down to drain on paper towel.

NUTRIENTS
(Average per teaspoon)
Energy 33 kJ (8 kCal)

Protein	0.05 g
Fat	0.00 g
Carbohydrate	1.93 g
Thiamin	0.00 mg
Riboflavin	0.00 mg
Niacin	0.01 mg
Vitamin C	1.44 mg
Calcium	0.43 mg
Iron	0.02 mg

LEMONADE OR ORANGEADE CONCENTRATE

from 18 months

Keep a screw-top jar of this fruit concentrate in the fridge as a handy treat for your toddler and little friends.

INGREDIENTS

4 medium lemons or 3 medium oranges
¾ cup castor sugar
2 tablespoons grated lemon or orange rind
¾ cup water

METHOD

1. Place oranges or lemons on edge of the turntable and microwave on HIGH (90–100%) for 1 minute. Remove and stand.
2. Combine sugar, lemon or orange rind and water in a 4-cup microwave-safe jug. Cover with plastic wrap, turning back an edge to vent.
3. Microwave on HIGH (90–100%), off the centre of the turntable, until all the sugar has dissolved.
4. Juice lemons or oranges and stir into syrup.
5. Store, covered, in the refrigerator. To serve, pour 1 tablespoon concentrate over ice and add 1 cup water.

VARIATION

- For the adventurous or advanced eater, garnish with finely chopped mint leaves.

POINTERS

- Heating individual pieces of citrus fruit in the microwave on HIGH (90–100%) for 30–40 seconds, then allowing to stand for 1 minute before squeezing, maximises the juice.
- Using a zester, you can grate rind from citrus fruit before squeezing out the juice. Ensure that the tart, white pith is left on the fruit.

NUTRIENTS
(Average per diluted cup)
Energy 170 kJ (41 kCal)

Nutrient	Amount
Protein	0.08 g
Fat	0.02 g
Carbohydrate	10.00 g
Thiamin	0.01 mg
Riboflavin	0.00 mg
Niacin	0.03 mg
Vitamin C	9.34 mg
Calcium	1.45 mg
Iron	0.03 mg

Party food

Children love parties, but they needn't be expensive or time-consuming if you use your microwave oven. All you need is a little imagination to cook Dinosaur Cake (p. 185) or Echidnas (p. 186); for something faster try Cocktail Frankfurts (p. 178) with the Big Dipper (p. 177).

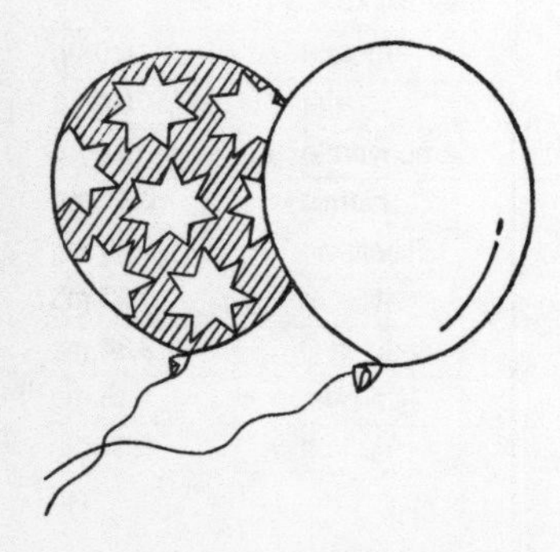

BIG DIPPER *from 18 months*

Fun for party-goers. Makes approximately 1 cup.

INGREDIENTS

2 quantities thick White Sauce (p. 145)
1 × 225 g can baked beans
1–2 tablespoons tomato sauce

METHOD

1. Prepare white sauce. If pre-made, warm in the microwave on HIGH (90–100%) for 1 minute to soften.
2. Purée sauce with baked beans and tomato sauce.
3. Serve with raw vegetables, toast or pitta chips.

VARIATIONS

- Add a little chilli sauce to taste.
- Use orange juice instead of tomato sauce.
- Use one whole, skinned tomato.

POINTER

- Dry a slice of pitta bread by splitting in two halves, placing on paper towel and microwaving on HIGH (90–100%) for 1½–2 minutes, turning over once. Cut into chips for dipping.

COCKTAIL FRANKFURTS

from 2 years

INGREDIENT

500 g cocktail frankfurts

METHOD

1. Rinse frankfurts well and separate. Pierce each frankfurt.
2. Place around the edge of a large microware container. Cover and vent.
3. Microwave on HIGH (90–100%) for 2 minutes. Rotate each frankfurt and microwave another 2 minutes on HIGH (90–100%).
4. Stand for 1 minute and serve with tomato sauce.

VARIATION

- Remove skin for smaller babies.

POINTER

- Heat 2 frankfurts only by wrapping in microwave-safe plastic wrap and microwaving on HIGH (90–100%) for 30 seconds, rotating halfway through cooking.

NUTRIENTS

(Average per frankfurt)

Energy 520 kJ (124 kCal)

Nutrient	Amount
Protein	7.15 g
Fat	9.95 g
Carbohydrate	1.70 g
Thiamin	0.06 mg
Riboflavin	0.06 mg
Niacin	0.85 mg
Vitamin C	0.00 mg
Calcium	16.50 mg
Iron	1.15 mg

CHICK PEA DIPPER WITH PITTA CHIPS

from 2 years

These round legumes have a slightly nutty but bland flavour. They make an excellent ingredient in soups and stews, and are the base of many familiar dips such as hummus.

INGREDIENTS

2 × 15 cm pitta breads
1 × 310 g can chick peas, drained
2 tablespoons mayonnaise
1 tablespoon Real Tomato Sauce (p. 150)

METHOD

1. Split pitta breads in half, to give 4 rounds. Cut each round into 12 wedges.
2. Place a piece of white paper towel on a roasting rack. Arrange 12 wedges around the edge, points towards the centre.
3. Microwave on HIGH (90–100%) for 1½ minutes.
4. Repeat with remaining wedges. Allow to cool and crispen.
5. Mash together well, or purée, chick peas, mayonnaise and tomato sauce.
6. Serve dip with pitta chips.

POINTERS

- Speed up the cooking of dried peas by covering with cold water, bringing to the boil on HIGH (90–100%) for 10–15 minutes, then simmering on DEFROST (30–35%) for 40–50 minutes. They will then be ready to use.
- Split pitta rounds can be microwaved whole and then broken into pieces when cold.

FRUIT TREATS *from 13 months*

Easy finger food for parties. Serves 8–10.

INGREDIENTS

100 g carob buttons
2 tablespoons melted butter
500 g mix of apples, pears and bananas, cut into 2-cm pieces
2 tablespoons butter, melted

METHOD

1. Place carob buttons into a 2-cup (500-ml) microwave-safe glass jug.
2. Place jug off the centre of the turntable and microwave on MEDIUM (50–60%) for 3–4 minutes, stirring several times, to melt.
3. Stir in melted butter and mix well.
4. Dip fruit pieces into carob mix.
5. Place fruit on foil-lined tray and refrigerate to set.
6. Serve as finger food.

VARIATION

- Use strawberries for older toddlers.

POINTER

- Melt butter in custard cup for 1 minute on MEDIUM (50–60%) so that it does not clarify.

NUTRIENTS
(Average per serve)
Energy 516 kJ (123 kCal)

Nutrient	Amount
Protein	1.52 g
Fat	7.27 g
Carbohydrate	13.37 g
Thiamin	0.02 mg
Riboflavin	0.03 mg
Niacin	0.11 mg
Vitamin C	4.35 mg
Calcium	15.91 mg
Iron	0.60 mg

FRUITY CHEWS *from 2 years*

Sweet and slightly crunchy temptations for parties. Makes 20.

INGREDIENTS

1 cup desiccated coconut
1 cup cornflakes
1 cup chopped dried fruit
1 × 200 g tube condensed milk

METHOD

1. Mix all ingredients together thoroughly. Shape into small balls.
2. Place a piece of baking paper on the turntable. Arrange 6 balls around the edge of the turntable, flatten lightly.
3. Microwave on HIGH (90–100%) for 1¾ minutes.
4. While still warm, re-shape with a knife or spatula, if necessary. Stand for 5 minutes before removing to cake racks to cool.
5. Repeat procedure with remaining mixture. Store in airtight containers.

POINTERS

- Cook 1 cookie for 20 seconds on HIGH (90–100%).
- Overloading the microwave with more than 8–9 biscuits at a time causes burning.

NUTRIENTS
(Average per biscuit)
Energy 307 kJ (73 kCal)

Nutrient	Amount
Protein	1.46 g
Fat	3.29 g
Carbohydrate	9.94 g
Thiamin	0.04 mg
Riboflavin	0.10 mg
Niacin	0.37 mg
Vitamin C	0.10 mg
Calcium	32.50 mg
Iron	0.58 mg

FRUITED CHOC CRACKLES

from 18 months

A variation on a children's classic, carob gives a slightly nutty flavour whilst dried fruit adds the natural sugar flavour. Makes 20.

INGREDIENTS

125 g copha, chopped
½ cup icing sugar
1 tablespoon carob powder
½ cup desiccated coconut
¼ cup dried apple, chopped
¼ cup sultanas
2 cups Rice Bubbles

METHOD

1. Melt copha in 4-litre ovenable jug on HIGH (90–100%) for 3 minutes. Stand for 5 minutes.
2. Sift icing sugar and carob into copha, mix well.
3. Add remaining ingredients, mix thoroughly.
4. Spoon into patty cases, pressing down lightly to pack.
5. Chill in freezer for 5 minutes to set quickly.

VARIATIONS

- Use cocoa in place of carob powder.
- Add other dried fruits of your choice.

POINTER

- Chop copha to enable it to melt easily.

NUTRIENTS
(Average per crackle)
Energy 452 kJ (108 kCal)

Nutrient	Amount
Protein	0.33 g
Fat	7.35 g
Carbohydrate	10.50 g
Thiamin	0.03 mg
Riboflavin	0.04 mg
Niacin	0.29 mg
Vitamin C	0.30 mg
Calcium	4.96 mg
Iron	0.40 mg

CAROB MOUSSE *from 12 months*

Carob powder or carob dots have a sweet chocolate flavour and look like cocoa powder or chocolate dots, but have a floury texture. They can be used as a substitute for cocoa or chocolate. Makes 4 serves.

INGREDIENTS

100 g carob buttons or dots
2 eggs, separated
rind of ½ orange
juice of 1 sweet orange
1–1½ teaspoons gelatine
grated carob for dusting

METHOD

1. Place carob buttons in 1-cup microwave-safe glass jug and microwave off the centre of the turntable on MEDIUM (50–60%) for 2–4 minutes, stirring several times.
2. Whisk in the egg yolks, stirring vigorously to see they do not scramble. Add orange rind.
3. Heat the orange juice and gelatine together in a small microwave container for 1 minute on HIGH (90–100%) until dissolved.
4. Add the carob mixture to the juice and cool in the refrigerator whilst preparing egg white.
5. Whisk egg whites in a clean glass bowl until stiff and dry. Fold into cooled carob mix. Divide mixture into 4 custard cups, chill for 30 minutes. Decorate with grated carob and serve.

VARIATION

- Chocolate buttons and grated chocolate can be used in place of carob.

POINTERS

- Have eggs at room temperature so carob doesn't set when yolks are added.
- Gelatine dissolves easily in the microwave. Mix with water or juice and cook on HIGH (90–100%) for 20–30 seconds.

NUTRIENTS
(Average per serve)
Energy 598 kJ (143 kCal)

Protein	3.65 g
Fat	2.52 g
Carbohydrate	26.37 g
Thiamin	0.03 mg
Riboflavin	0.22 mg
Niacin	0.26 mg
Vitamin C	14.36 mg
Calcium	98.11 mg
Iron	1.60 mg

HOT BANANA SUNDAE

from 2 years

Marshmallows are fun to watch grow when heated in a microwave oven, and to watch collapse at the end of cooking time!

INGREDIENTS

1 banana
3 marshmallows
choc bits or dots

METHOD

1. Split skin of banana open but leave on. Place marshmallows on banana between skin and sprinkle with a few choc dots.
2. Place on the edge of the turntable. Microwave on HIGH (90–100%) for 30 seconds.
3. Serve in a dish with a scoop of ice cream.

VARIATION

- Use carob bits instead of choc bits.

POINTER

- A fun party trick with marshmallows is to place a few in the microwave oven and heat for 2-3 minutes on HIGH (90-100%). They grow huge and, whilst they are inedible, children love watching them grow.

NUTRIENTS
(Average per serve)
Energy 1251 kJ (299 kCal)

Protein	5.18 g
Fat	8.25 g
Carbohydrate	52.92 g
Thiamin	0.11 mg
Riboflavin	0.27 mg
Niacin	0.58 mg
Vitamin C	16.80 mg
Calcium	89.45 mg
Iron	0.94 mg

DINOSAUR CAKE *from 2 years*

Dinosaurs are favourites with kids of all ages. Serves 8.

INGREDIENTS
125 g butter
½ cup castor sugar
1 cup self-raising flour
2 tablespoons custard powder
2 eggs
2 tablespoons milk

METHOD

1. Melt butter in a medium microwave jug or bowl on HIGH (90–100%) for 45 seconds.
2. Add sugar, mix well. Add remaining ingredients. Stir well with a fork until combined.
3. Line a ring pan with white paper towel. Pour mixture in. Place on a rack or inverted saucer and microwave on HIGH (90–100%) for 3½ minutes.
4. Stand directly on bench and cover with paper towel for 5 minutes.
5. Turn out and remove paper to cool completely.
6. Cut cake in half to form two semi-circles. Place on serving plate and decorate with green icing and dried fruit or lollies for eyes. Use lolly bananas, cut in half, for the spikes down its back and licorice for its feet.

VARIATION

- 'Okay For Kids' Chocolate Cake (p. 158) can be substituted if a darker cake is preferred.
- Alternatively, cake can lie down for a snake, or join curves together for a butterfly.

NUTRIENTS
(Average per slice)
Energy 1056 kJ (252 kCal)

Protein	3.47 g
Fat	14.44 g
Carbohydrate	27.36 g
Thiamin	0.05 mg
Riboflavin	0.06 mg
Niacin	0.22 mg
Vitamin C	0.05 mg
Calcium	32.39 mg
Iron	0.40 mg

ECHIDNAS (OR HAY STACKS)

from 2 years

Packets of ready-to-serve fried egg noodles are widely available and are a wonderful snack on their own, or make them into party treats! Makes 20–24.

INGREDIENTS
100 g unsalted butter
1/4 cup chocolate hazelnut spread
100 g fried noodles

METHOD
1. Melt butter in a medium casserole dish on HIGH (90–100%) for 1 minute.
2. Add chocolate hazelnut spread and mix until smooth.
3. Add noodles, mix thoroughly. Spoon small amounts onto a foil or baking paper lined tray. Press together lightly.
4. Chill to set. Serve chilled.

VARIATION
- Use unsalted smooth peanut butter.

POINTERS
- Chop butter into small pieces for easy melting.
- Overheating butter when melting will clarify it.

NUTRIENTS
(Average per echidna)
Energy 320 kJ (76 kCal)

Protein	0.60 g
Fat	6.63 g
Carbohydrate	3.94 g
Thiamin	0.01 mg
Riboflavin	0.01 mg
Niacin	0.03 mg
Vitamin C	0.00 mg
Calcium	12.03 mg
Iron	0.10 mg

GENERAL INDEX

INDEX OF RECIPES

INDEX OF HINTS

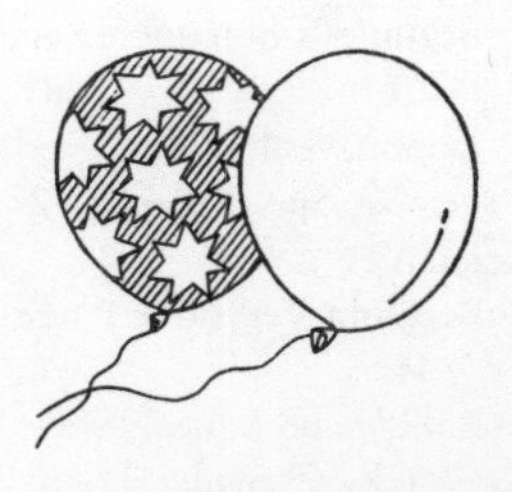